Advances in Psychology Series

PSYCHOLOGICAL PROBABILITY

In the same series

JOHN COHEN

Psychological
Probability
or The Art of Doubt

SCHENKMAN PUBLISHING COMPANY
CAMBRIDGE, MASSACHUSETTS

Distributed by General Learning Press

Schenkman books are distributed by
General Learning Press
250 James Street
Morristown, New Jersey 07960

© *George Allen & Unwin Ltd.,* 1973

First published in the United States by
Schenkman Publishing Company
Cambridge, Massachusetts 1973

Library of Congress Catalog Card Number: 72-81521
Printed in the United States

To Cyril Burt

PREFACE

This book was prompted by a request to participate in a Symposium on Statistical Causality organised by the Niels Bohr Institute of Theoretical Physics at the University of Copenhagen, to celebrate the fiftieth anniversary of the founding of the Institute. At the suggestion of Professor Leon Rosenfeld, the paper I presented was entitled 'Perceptive Probability' (by analogy with Michotte's 'perception of causality'). I have taken the opportunity to amplify this paper and present it to the reader together with papers on closely related topics, as an introduction to the study of 'psychological probability'.

I am aware that some academic psychologists demur at the intrusion of historical and literary references (e.g. Chapter 8) in a book which purports to be scientific. Their misgiving is justified, I feel, only if all sources are treated on a par, with respect to the validity of the 'evidence' they offer. To my way of thinking, everything is grist to the psychological mill. The kind of psychology which I should like to see develop is one which is not only deeply rooted in the biological sciences and mathematically sound, but also has a close affinity to social studies and the humanities. If there is such a thing as psychology, it should consist (to paraphrase Bertrand Russell) of propositions which do not occur in any other discipline.

In what is, after all, intended to be a general sketch of a field of investigation as a whole, rather than a detailed treatment of the parts of this field, it is perhaps not easy to perceive the unity of the book as it stands. Nevertheless, a unity there undoubtedly is intended to be, and the exposition will be at fault if this is not sensed by the reader.

So far as the structure of the text is concerned, the first four chapters are designed to treat basic issues and concepts: information in relation to probability, psychologically considered; the role of language in expressing and conveying ideas of probability, and the central and fundamental part which the ideas of chance, independence, sampling and inference, again psychologically considered, play in the subject as a whole. In order to give flesh to the bones of theoretical concepts, an outline is given of experimental studies, together with their results, of chance, independence and sampling.

At the same time, I have felt it necessary, at the end of Chapter 2, to dwell a little on certain inescapable philosophical implications of the study of subjective chance. And towards the end of Chapter 4, I have tried to bring out into open discussion certain analogies which might be drawn between psychology and physics. In particular, I have ventured to draw the attention of students of personality and related topics to the implications for them of the ideas set forth in Chapter 4.

The second half of the book (Chapters 5 to 8) is devoted to illustrating the manner in which the theoretical ideas earlier adumbrated enter into a selected range of beliefs, practices and professional procedures, as well as in the literary treatment of love and drama, and in the appreciation of art—these last topics being somewhat alien to the usual psychological text. If, therefore, the first half of the book may be described as 'theoretical', the second part may be roughly described as 'applied', although this second part also proposes specific models of gambling behaviour, the transmission of effective information in medicine, and criminal conduct, respectively.

I would, accordingly, like to persuade the reader that the book is, or endeavours to be, an organic whole, and not a patchwork of unrelated chapters, though I may not succeed in doing so.

In a sense all the chapters, in one way or another, are concerned with the interpretation of subjective uncertainty, and with the manifestation, in word and deed, of this interpretation. I am therefore not occupied with inaccessible private experience, but with communicable and, generally, measurable aspects of this experience.

The continuity may be rendered slightly more plain and convincing by making explicit the implicit links between the successive chapters. Having, in Chapter 1, begun at what seemed to me to be the beginning, and dealt with preliminary considerations affecting the use of language and intuition, Chapter 2 takes up what I consider to be the central concepts which have to be examined experimentally, namely, independence and chance. This leads, in Chapter 3, to recent experiments on the psychological compounding of chances in a situation of sequential choice. From here we move, in Chapter 4, with the idea of chance still in mind, but rather in the background, to confront the question of inference, 'deductively' from population to sample, and 'inductively' from sample to population. This discussion, provisional though it may be, of independence, chance, and inference, paves the way for a study of the interpretation of uncertainty in selected situations and predicaments. Gambling, in Chapter 5, seems a particularly appropriate topic to illustrate the way the various elements in subjective uncertainty—chance, luck, hope, characteristic misjudgement—combine with developmental and emotional features to generate a state of mind of great complexity. But the idea of a gamble is not limited to horse-racing and the roulette table. In a disguised form it enters into the beliefs we acquire relating to health and disease. Hence, Chapter 6 explores the influence of ideas of chance, especially in relation to credibility and action, both from the point of view of the doctor and from the point of view of the patient. It seems logical enough, in Chapter 7, to attempt what partly amounts to the same type of analysis in the sphere of crime. Just as there is an analogue between the doctor's examination and the detective's interrogation, so the patient's fear of illness may be compared with an offender's anxiety of being caught and punished.

Finally, in Chapter 8, I have taken the liberty to wander a little further afield, particularly in view of my belief that the student of psychology has much to learn from a reading of literature and from some familiarity with trends in art. But at this point I address myself to a rather wider audience, those who might desire to seek to throw a ray of psychological light on otherwise obscure aspects of literature.

I am deeply grateful to Sir Cyril Burt for several very helpful comments and suggestions. My thanks are also due to the Kunsthistorisches Museum, Vienna, for permission to reproduce Van Mieris's 'The Doctor's Visit'; to the Arp Estate and Messrs Thames & Hudson for permission to reproduce Jean Arp's 'Rectangles arranged according to the Laws of Chance'; to the editor of *Nebelspalter* and Mr Hans Haëm for permission to reproduce a cartoon by the latter; and finally to my secretary, Mrs Nora Partridge, for expert care and devotion in typing the manuscript.

CONTENTS

ILLUSTRATIONS

GRAPHS

TABLES

CHAPTER 1

Perception of Probability

I. *The Postman's Paradox*

The 'perception' of probability is a mode of apprehending the world by conjecture. But what do we mean by 'apprehend'?, by 'the world'? by 'conjecture'? Suppose we take 'apprehend' to denote some kind of information processing, together with a degree of assent to the information thus processed. We can still ask what is the nature of the 'information'? and what is the character of the 'processing'? It cannot be taken for granted, to begin with, that we register information in the same amount and form as it is transmitted to us. Such a view presupposes a model of perception which conceives of information entering the mind (or brain) as a fish enters a factory to be turned into paste. This is too simple a representation of the interface between the perceiver and his world. We may provisionally have to assume, not a two-stage model, namely, 'perceiving' followed by processing, but a single-stage model in which processing is inherent in the very act of apprehension. The human brain seems to act like a fish-canning factory which processes the fish before, in fact, they reach the factory. Or like a man who must open and read his letter before the postman delivers it; the postman only being able to deliver it, since the address is inside, after it has been opened and read by the recipient.[1]

I have ventured to introduce this paradoxical model advisedly, in order to bring home the complexity of the situation with which we are confronted in the simplest forms of perception, which is characterized by three main features. First, it is mediated by the antennae-like function of the senses. We have to imagine that, for example, our eye-balls extrude from the head, each on its 'stalk', and seek their objectives, which are interpreted by us at the very moment they are visually seized. Our ears are to be conceived as behaving in a similar fashion. Secondly, the senses are social organs; they transmit and receive messages with a social impact. Thirdly, they function intermodally. It is in this context that we must try to understand the 'perception' of probability.

II. *Information and Processing*

'Information' is commonly assumed to be exclusively 'selective'. But there are forms of 'information' which cannot be characterized in this way, such as, for example, semantic, aesthetic and what, for want of a better word, might be called 'inventive' information. 'Selective' information is a logarithmic measure of the improbability of the occurrence of an event, or of a message, in a given situation. As such, it represents only one of the measurable aspects of the event or the message, namely, the statistical aspect.

Semantic information has to do with the meaning of sentences. Sometimes it is defined as the class of all the sentences (in a particular linguistic system) which follow logically from a given sentence; sometimes it is defined as the class of all the content elements which follow from a given sentence.

While there undoubtedly are statistical, selective elements in aesthetic information, both in the creation and in the appreciation of a work of art, no one would claim that such elements exhaust the aesthetic character of a work of art. And much the same may be said of 'inventive' information in art, science, technology or other spheres of human activity. It would be difficult, for example, to reduce the manner whereby Newton arrived at his laws of motion, or their content, to selective operations.

When we speak of 'apprehending' as the processing of information, we must reckon with a subjective counterpart of selective information; and by 'subjective' I do not mean 'incommunicable'. This counterpart may be measured in terms of the number of binary questions an individual needs to ask in order to gain one 'bit' of selective information. The need to measure subjective information in this sense arises from the fact that, as I have said, in human communication, the amount of selective information received is not necesarily the same as the amount transmitted. The discrepancy is attributable to limitations in 'channel capacity', as well as to the existence of prior distributions and special 'weighting functions' characteristic of the individual receiver. Thus, we have to substitute psychological probabilities $\{\psi_1, \ldots, \psi_n\}$ for the statistical probabilities $\{p_1, \ldots, p_n\}$.

As to the question of 'processing', here we have to allow for a large class of activities, some conscious and some non-conscious (which is not the same as 'unconscious' in a Freudian sense). There is no reason to suppose that all conscious processes are logical, and all non-conscious processes alogical or illogical. Conscious processes include logical operations, varying in complexity, such as classifying, ordering, generalizing and inferring, as well as day-dreaming and fantasy. On the other hand, non-conscious processes include not only contiguous association, analogical thinking, and metaphor-making, but also logical problem-solving (during sleep or dreams) and innovation. The search for words in speech and composition is pre-eminently a non-conscious affair which may involve, at the same time, both logical and alogical features.

Finally, by apprehending 'the world', I mean the world of everyday things, while 'conjecture' denotes varieties of guessing. The capacity to guess correctly may have been an important factor in evolution, by favouring the survival of organisms which match their 'expectations' to actuality; in other words, we might say, by their perception of statistical causality. Biologically, therefore, perceptive probability may be said to be a feature of man and animal alike, in so far as it guides the response to the relative frequency of an event. No doubt, as Keynes[2] remarks, it would take a dog a long time to find out that he was given scraps (of meat) every day except on fast days, and that there was the same number of these in each year. All the same, a dog, like the members of many other species, is capable of 'probability learning', that is to say, of learning, by reward, to fit the frequency of a response to the frequency of an event. Furthermore, a habit acquired by an animal as a result of intermittent reward tends to be more resistant to extinction than a habit established by continuous reward. So we may say that, at a humbler level, perceptive probability in some sense governs the animal, as it does the human, kingdom. In human learning, the frequency of a binary response may be matched with the frequency of a given binary event even without a reward for the appropriate response. The introduction of a reward tends to induce a 'maximization strategy', in which the subject invariably gives the response appropriate to the more frequent event.[3]

The word *perceptive*, however, suggests that which is mediated by our senses. There is also a *conceptual* probability, which, though equally subjective, is more abstract and not directly or immediately connected with what we see, hear, smell or touch. So it might be better to speak of *psychological* probability, which embraces both sub-sets—the perceptive and the conceptual.

III. *Descriptive Theory*

The theory of psychological probability is not prescriptive. It does not tell us how to reason when we are in doubt or when our knowledge is incomplete. Nor is it a normative logic or partial belief. It is a descriptive theory of the mind at work, and its aim is to determine the principles which govern judgement in uncertainty. It is not, therefore, in competition with other interpretations of probability.[4] Nor does it assert that all probabilities are merely 'in the head'. On the contrary, if guidance is needed in decision-making or action, probabilities 'in the head' must be supplemented or corrected by probabilities which are not merely 'in the head', though it is only when we have established the range and nature of psychological probabilities that we can attempt to correct or optimize them.

The species of probability of which I speak is not to be confused with the varieties of subjective probability in its axiomatic treatment, as part of statistical decision theory, Bayesian or other. Subjective probability is commonly taken to be an assessment of a probability, or a degree of belief in an event or a proposition, which can be expressed as a number between 0 and 1. On this view, if the probability assessed is consistent with certain reasonable postulates of behaviour, it is said to correspond to 'a probability measure'. But a degree of belief, expressed as a number between 0 and 1, is only one of the many flora and fauna of psychological probability. Essentially, it is a second-order value (ψ_2) indicating a degree of confidence in a first-order judgement (ψ_1).

L. J. Savage[5] states that subjective probability refers to the opinion of an idealized person as reflected by his behaviour, real or potential. This idealized person 'never makes mistakes, never gives thirteen pence for a shilling, or makes such a combination of bets that he is sure to lose, no matter what happens'. Furthermore, the role of subjective probability in statistics is 'to make statistics less subjective'. What I call perceptive (or, better, psychological) probability refers to the behaviour and judgements of real people, who do make mistakes, such as giving thirteen pence for a shilling or betting in such a way that they are bound to lose. These very *mistakes* are part of my subject-matter. The aim of Savage and his fellow 'subjective probabilists' is to prevent people from errant behaviour by showing them how to be consistent with their own 'true' desires. I have no such normative aim. I suspect, too, that until we have a well-documented natural history of human error, such as the study of psychological probability can give us, the contribution that the subjectivist school can make towards the elimination of human error will be rather limited.

IV. *Language of Probability*

Before coming to the heart of the matter, which has to do with the way we conceive of independence and chance, let us try and pierce the haze of words in which these and kindred ideas are enveloped. How do people come to use language about probability in the way they do? We can ask the same question about the language of causality, and Michotte's famous experiments themselves appear to need reassessing in the light of this question. There is a class of words and phrases which may be described as being precisely inexact. 'Probably', 'likely', 'might happen', 'sure', are examples; and there are sub-sets relating to magnitude, space, time and other basic categories. Such expressions are potentially quantifiable, and the ratios of pairs of appropriate values assigned to them, in a given context, at different ages, show a clear linear trend from infancy to maturity. For instance, the ratio of 'often' to 'rarely', in terms of the numerical values assigned to them, ranges from approximately unity at age 5 to 20 at maturity.[6]

The age effect which leads to greater numerical discrimination is related to the fact that sets which adults treat as non-intersecting, are treated by children as intersecting, or as overlapping distributions. Thus the younger the child the more likely he is to say that a big dwarf is larger than a small giant. For him the attribute is dominant over the noun, partly because he treats the words 'big' and 'small' as absolute rather than as relative to dwarf and giant, in the same way as he treats 'a few of' or 'many' to some extent as equivalent to absolute numbers.

We seem to have here a fundamental duality: the child cannot use the word 'probably' correctly until he understands the underlying idea, yet he cannot grasp this idea until he knows the meaning of the word. This sort of duality bedevils the more fundamental question of the acquisition of speech.

But it is not only children who cause us some puzzlement in their use of the language of probability. Consider the following statement by a Nobel laureate:

Unilateral disarmament by the Western Powers 'would certainly very considerably increase the probability of such a catastrophe (i.e. World War III)'.[7]

Without entering into the substantive issues let us try to divine what the statement is intended to convey. It seems to be saying three things, viz.

(a) there is a probability of World War III
(b) this probability would be considerably increased by unilateral disarmament
(c) it is certain that (b)

Consider (a), (b) and (c) in turn. (a) there is a probability of World War III may be taken to express a degree of belief, or subjective probability (ψ). Since the event (E) in question, World War III, is not repeatable, it would not be proper to regard (a) as an assertion of a physical probability based on relative frequency. We may represent (a) as:

$$\psi_1(E) > 0.$$

(b) is an assertion that this prior probability would increase to a larger value in an assumed posterior probability (after unilateral disarmament). If so, we could represent (b) as:

$$\dot\psi_1 > \psi_1$$

where $\dot\psi_1$ is the assumed posterior degree of belief.

Finally (c) 'it is certain that (b)', is a higher order degree of belief. If we take (b) to be a simple assertion, 'would be', (c) could be represented as:

$$\psi_2 [\dot\psi_1 > \psi_1] \to 1.$$

Take this further example of the way in which the idea of chance, presumably to convey probability, enters into a public pronouncement. According to a report[8] published in July 1969, Mr Harold Wilson, the then British Prime Minister, stated that he reckoned Labour had 'a better than even chance of winning the next election'. What exactly did he mean by this? Did he mean that if the election were to be held an indefinitely large number of times under the same conditions, Labour would be triumphant on, say, 55 per cent of the occasions? Did he mean that, taking all the ponderables and imponderables into account (wages, prices, the Common Market, foreign policy) a statistical prediction would favour Labour at the next election? Or did he mean nothing more than that he himself was in less than complete doubt about the outcome, thus projecting his feelings on to the actual situation? If this last supposition is correct, Mr Wilson provides an illustration of what we mean by 'subjective chance'.

A similar announcement was made in 1970, this time in the name of the Senate Republican leader who is reported[9] to have stated that there was a '50–50 chance' that an agreement to freeze the number of strategic missiles would be accepted by the US and the USSR. Did he mean that whether agreement would be reached or not would be (or could be) decided by the toss of a coin? Did he mean that if the deliberations were to be repeated a large number of times, agreement would be reached, on the average, on half the occasions? Or did he mean that he had no idea at all whether agreement would be reached or not, and therefore felt prepared to take an even bet, expressing this state of ignorance in the language of the betting man 'there is a 50–50 chance'?

The point of giving these illustrations is not to insist on imposing on them one particular interpretation, but to draw attention to the manner in which the expression and communication of ideas, about which there can be some legitimate doubt, is characteristic even of men of highly trained intellect. It therefore seems legitimate to enquire into the precise signification of these ideas and, also, to ask whether they are grounded in some conception of probability.

V. *Intuitionism*

This brings us to the problem of intuitionism. What elements, if any, in the idea of probability are given, so to speak, by the 'constitution' of the human mind (and brain), and what elements are culturally determined? The considerable diversity among mathematical statisticians and logicians as to the interpretation of the idea of probability should make us pause before making any categorical assertions about intuitive probability. And we should also hesitate before making such statements as 'the theory of probability as a mathematical science must be based on certain premises *that represent a generalization of centuries-old* experience'[10] (my italics).

The belief that the idea of probability is given, and owes nothing to experience, has a long history. We find it clearly enunciated by Lord Herbert of Cherbury early in the seventeenth century.[11] He included it among the Common Notions. Those Notions which are not self-evident are 'probable'. They include 'every assertion which has not been fully understood, examined, recognized and brought into connection with other assertions of the same order'. This probability, for Herbert, included anything derived from mere visual observation, and hence, most of astronomy. Anything which rests on hearsay, the 'specious assumptions of medical men, all the crude and hasty ideas and opinions produced by the tricks of orators, all incoherent dogmas, and all similar beliefs which cannot clearly be accepted or rejected, must be classed as probable'. Probability, which is akin to possibility and falsity, is contrasted with truth. In this context, probability has a pejorative flavour, and the fact that it is a Common Notion does not grant it the status of an innate and true idea.

As is well known, Koopman[12] (1940) takes an extreme view when he states that experience is to be interpreted in terms of probability, rather than the other way round; a primal intuition, he asserts, enables us to order eventualities. This seems tantamount to saying that intuitive probability is innate, a kind of Kantian category. The most we can concede, I think, is a perceptive probability at a biological level. If we go beyond this, we may reveal our ignorance rather than our knowledge. For unless we follow the method of Socrates, in the *Meno*, when he tried to demonstrate that the proof of Pythagoras's theorem is 'known' even to an illiterate youth, we cannot assume that an understanding of conceptual probability is 'wired into' the brain. And it has yet to be shown that maturation, *per se*, without reference to experience and learning, is a sufficient explanation.

In principle, Koopman's view does not differ very much from Borel's claim that 'the notion of probability is a primitive one whose significance everyone grasps intuitively'[13] Nor does it seem basically different from the 'intuitive notion of probability' assumed by some advocates of the frequency interpretation. Thus Feller[14] declares that this presumed intuitive notion is based on the assumption that:

'If in *n* identical trials *A* occurs *m* times, and if *n* is very large, then *m/n* should be the probability of *A*'.

But this seems circular. For what is the 'probability of *A*'? Either, I suppose, 'the number of times *A* occurs in *n* trials', or it is a parameter of which *m/n* is an estimate. If so, in both cases the 'probability of *A*' is arbitrarily defined. Of course, there is nothing wrong in making arbitrary assumptions, so long as these are explicit. What Feller seems to me to be saying, however, (if I am not misinterpreting him) is that our intuitive notion of probability is based on an assumption which itself envolves the self-same intuitive notion. If the intuitive notion is logically different from the assumption, we should be told wherein the difference lies, and how the former rests on the latter.[15]

Strictly speaking, a statement to the effect that '*x*' is 'intuitive' ought to be based on psychological evidence. The statement in question is neither self-evident nor supported by mathematical considerations. Other difficulties, which cannot be resolved by appeal to observation or, indeed, to logic, arise over the interpretation of probability. Thus the logical interpretation of Keynes seemed so alien to Borel[16] that he came to the conclusion that British and Continental minds are differently constructed, and that this difference should be treated as 'a matter of fact'. Borel conceded that the logical interpretation is 'incontestable in principle', but maintained that one may sometimes speak directly of the probability of an event. For a physicist, he asserted, 'the probability that an atom of radium will explode tomorrow is . . . a constant of the same kind as the density of copper or the atomic weight of gold'. Nevertheless, he favoured the bet as a measure of probability and he envisaged the study of simple games of chance which would form the basis of a new science 'where psychology will be no less useful than mathematics'.

A view similar to Feller's is taken by Gnedenko.[17] But he introduces novel sentiments when he declares that the views of Soviet theorists have developed along Marxist-Leninist lines, and have crystallized 'in a severe struggle between materialistic and idealistic conceptions'. And it is (he suggests) because of their idealistic conceptions 'painstakingly camouflaged with the words experiment, practice, and natural science', that von Mises and others have been 'openly opposed to the elemental materialistic views' of J. Bernoulli, Laplace and the Soviet mathematicians, according to whom the theory of probability 'reflects the laws inherent in random events of nature'.

It is only fair to add that other mathematical statisticians, of equal distinction, do not share this view, and even regard it as metaphysical. De Finetti,[18] for instance, insists that to him the subjective interpretation is the only meaningful one.

It is instructive to note that de Finetti supports his case by drawing an analogy with the impact of quantum theory on classical physics. Just as quantum theory, with its probabilistic interpretations of micro-events, was at first regarded as a threat to determinism and 'the whole edifice of science', so subjective probability, he argues, is regarded by advocates of 'objective probability' with the same sort of suspicion. In both situations, he asserts, a radical revision of ideas is essential for the advance of science. A dispute of this order which cannot be resolved by a crucial experiment cannot be regarded as scientific but as doctrinal.

I conclude by reiterating, for emphasis, that a better understanding of perceptive probability will rest on (i) a clarification of the kindred notions of 'information' and 'processing'; (ii) a better understanding of the language of probability in everyday life as well as in scientific discourse; and (iii) a resolution of the dispute of intuitionism v. empiricism in the treatment of the fundamental idea.

APPENDIX 1

The psychological value of a bit of selective information may be measured in terms of the number of binary questions an individual needs to ask in order to gain one bit of selective information. By way of illustration, consider the simple task of locating a target in an array of four possible targets, in which case two bits of selective information are required. One person might ask, in turn, in respect to three of the four possible targets: 'Is it this one?', and each time receive the answer 'No'. The first 'No' conveys [$\log_2 4 - \log_2 3$ (= 0·42)] bits. The second 'No' conveys [$\log_2 3 - \log_2 2$ (= 0·58)] bits. The third 'No' conveys $\log_2$ (= 1) bit. This person has asked three questions to gain two bits. He may think that, in successively eliminating three of the four possible targets, he is making three equal mental steps towards the goal, although, in fact, each 'No' provides him unwittingly with a relatively greater amount of selective information.

A second person might ask 'Is it one of these two?' and receive the answer 'No', which conveys [$\log_2 4 - \log_2 2$ (= 1)] bit. He then asks: 'Is it this one (of the remaining two)?', and once more receives the reply 'No', which again yields $\log_2 2$ (= 1) bit. He asks two questions to gain the same amount of information as the first person, but he may think he is making unequal steps towards the target.

The designation 'item' has been proposed, as a psychological measure of subjective information, to refer to the number of questions asked by an individual to gain one bit of selective information. The reciprocal relation, namely the number of bits gained by one binary question, may be regarded as a measure of the efficiency of the question.

APPENDIX 2

In 1970, the interpretation of 'probability' arose in the context of London's tidal-flooding defence schemes. The leader of the Greater London Council, Desmond Plummer, maintained that the flooding of square miles of Central London and a quarter million people was 'imminent'. Lord Kennet, Parliamentary Secretary at the Ministry of Housing, challenged this view. He is reported to have said[19] that 'the chance of serious flooding in London was 100 to 1'. Was this another way of saying that flooding occurs in London, on the average, once in a hundred years? If so, it might be misleading to represent the odds as applying to any particular year, regardless of the state of tide and wind. What would we think of a student who had not prepared himself for an examination and who consoled himself with the reflection that the failure rate, in the past, was one per cent? The apparent precision and objectivity of Lord Kennet's statement might lead the unwary to suppose that the chance of flooding in London in 1970 was, in fact, the same as the chance of picking the single winning ticket in one draw from a lottery of 101 tickets.

On the other hand, Lord Kennet might simply have been expressing his personal confidence that a flood would not take place, the odds '100 to 1' being nothing more than a way of indicating this. If that was his intention, it might have been wiser for him to say that 'a flood was not imminent'. For when the hazard is of such a magnitude —55 square miles and 1,200,000 people exposed to flooding—the projection of a personal belief as if it were a statistical reality is hard to justify.

The leader of the Greater London Council, likewise, may have attached a high personal probability to flooding just because it would be so dreadful if it *did* happen. His 'imminent' might reflect his feeling of horror rather than the 'true' statistical likelihood, whatever that might be.

NOTES

1 One of my bright students (Peter Coles) has remarked that the 'Postman's Paradox' raises an insuperable difficulty for contemporary theories of selective attention in relation to memory. For an individual must necessarily encode his environment meaningfully before he can selectively attend to particular features of it, and yet the process of encoding itself presupposes attentiveness.

2 J. M. Keynes, *A Treatise on Probability*, London: Macmillan, 1921, p. 332.

3 R. D. Luce and P. Suppes, 'Preference, Utility and Subjective Probability', in *Handbook of Mathematical Psychology* (R. D. Luce, R. R. Bush and E. Galanter, eds), New York: Wiley, 1965.

4 For a simple account of these interpretations, the reader is referred to Chapter 2 of *Information and Choice* (J. Cohen and I. Christensen), Edinburgh: Oliver & Boyd, 1970.

5 L. J. Savage *et al.*, *The Foundations of Statistical Inference*, London: Methuen, 1962

6 In some persons afflicted with schizophrenia we find that the words may be given an extraordinary exactitude. A patient told me that 'many friends' means 'exactly seventeen', and another said that 'hardly any trees in the park' means 'three and a half trees'.

7 E. B. Chain, 'Social Responsibility and the Scientist', *New Scientist*, 22 October 1970, p. 178.

8 The *Guardian*, 26 July 1969.

9 The *Guardian*, 22 May 1970.

10 B. V. Gnedenko, *The Theory of Probability* (trans. B. D. Seckler), New York: Chelsea Pub. Co., 1963, p. 52.

11 Herbert of Cherbury, *De Veritate* (1624) (trans. E. Carré), Bristol: University of Bristol Press, 1937, p. 319.

12 B. O. Koopman, 'The Axioms and Algebra of Intuitive Probability', *Ann. Math.*, 1940, Vol. 41, pp. 269–92.

13 É. Borel, *Probabilities and Life* (trans. M. Baudin), New York: Dover, 1962, p. 38 (first published 1942).

14 W. Feller, *An Introduction to Probability Theory and Its Applications*, New York: Wiley, 1966, 2nd ed., Vol. I, p. 141.

15 The agony which someone must feel if forced to articulate a primitive notion is exemplified in this reply given by a 10-year-old girl to the question: 'What does the sentence "It will *probably* rain" mean?' She said, 'It means: it will most likely rain; I suppose it will rain; I think it will rain; I am not sure it will rain; I am not certain it will rain; I do not know whether it will rain or not; I should think it will rain; it will rain I suppose.'

16 É. Borel, 'À propos d'un traité de probabilités', Note II of *Valeur pratique et philosophie des probabilités*, Paris: Gauthier-Villars, 1939, pp. 134–46 (a review of Keynes's *Treatise*, first published in *Revue philosophique*, 1924, Vol. 98, pp. 321–36.

17 Op. cit.

18 B. de Finetti, 'Logical Foundations and Measurement of Subjective Probability', *Acta Psychol.*, 1970, Vol. 34, pp. 129–45.

19 The *Guardian*, 21 January 1970.

CHAPTER 2

Independence and Chance

I. *Interpretations of 'Independence'*

Central to most interpretations of probability is the idea of independence, itself almost inseparable from the notion of randomness. Independence may be variously defined. An intuitive definition might be as follows: two events, x and y, are felt to be independent if the chance of x and y occurring together is the same as the chance of x occurring in the absence of y, or *vice versa*: x and y are independent if the probability of xy is the same as the probability of $x\bar{y}$. These two events, x and y, may be said to be *physically* independent if the proportion of x's among the y's is the same as it is among the non-y's. For example, if x denotes 'being infected' and y denotes 'being inoculated', x and y are physically independent if the proportion infected among the inoculated is the same as the proportion infected among the non-inoculated. In terms of *frequency*, x and y are said to be independent if the probability of finding them together is the product of the probabilities of finding either of them separately: $p(xy) = p(x) \times p(y)$. Finally, independence may be defined in terms of our knowledge (the logical interpretation): x and y are independent if knowledge of the existence of one provides no indication of anything which might be the cause or partly the cause of the other.[1]

There is no question of asserting that one or other of these definitions is psychologically privileged. The psychologist's task is rather to try to discover, first, how an understanding of these various interpretations of independence grows with increase in age, from childhood to adulthood, and secondly, to examine any systematic departures from these interpretations.

We can attempt to arrive at such an understanding by presenting to a subject a binary event which can have one of two mutually exclusive and equiprobable outcomes. How is this understood by him? Having witnessed some outcomes, how does this affect his prediction of the next outcome?

II. Development of the Idea of Independence

Now the idea of 'independence', in the sense of treating the next two possible outcomes as equiprobable, does not emerge suddenly in the adult mind. It undergoes a continuous elaboration through the period of intellectual development. Let us sketch this development. Suppose a child of six years of age witnesses a sequence of outcomes of a binary event, each outcome being independent of its predecessor, and he has to predict the next outcome at each stage in the sequence. The most marked feature at this age is a tendency to alternate from the previous prediction. To the extent that the child does not alternate, he tends to predict the outcome which has so far occurred less frequently than the other. He defends this guess by saying that it (i.e. the occurrence of the non-preponderant outcome) would be 'fair'. At this age, alternation tends to occur after *success* rather than after *failure*. If, for instance, a child guesses Black (or on the Right side) correctly, he expects the next outcome to be White (or on the Left side). But if he guesses Black (or on the Right side) incorrectly, he persists in predicting Black (or on the Right side) as before, which in effect means that he expects the next outcome to differ from its predecessor. We shall see later that similar phenomena, though in a reverse direction, are encountered in gambling. There is an inclination on the part of the adult player to believe that the wheel will change its winning colour at the next turn, but this tendency is more marked after an incorrect guess (loss) than after a correct guess (gain). On the whole, then, at this tender age children base their guesses almost entirely on the pattern of their previous guesses.

A year later, at the age of 7+, the tendency to guess the previously non-preponderant outcome becomes rather more pronounced. The child is now less affected by his previous choice, by success or failure in that choice or by whether he thinks he has been lucky. His guess begins to be clearly affected by the event outcomes, and he responds more to what is actually happening. Generally speaking, below the age of 10+, few children can distinguish outcomes which are 'truly' independent (in the sense of one of the three definitions given above) from those which are, or may be, partly dependent on previous outcomes, such as the weather on a particular day or the sex of an unborn child.

The idea of independence, as expressed in the judgement 'either outcome may occur', only emerges at the age of 12+. Henceforward, the tendency to predict non-preponderant outcomes is much weaker. The belief in luck now merges to some extent with the notion of chance. But the idea of dependence continues to be held, even by the same person, in two forms. In one form it favours a continuation of similar outcomes. In another form it favours the non-preponderant outcome; that is, there is a negative recency effect.[2]

In this connection it may be noted that adults do not seem able to select a random sequence from a set of random and non-random sequences. Their selection is biased towards a preference for the non-preponderant. Experiments have been so designed to rule out the possibility that the bias is due to a limitation in short-term memory or to a lapse of attention. Furthermore, binary sequences with conditional probabilities of the order of 0·4 are interpreted as more 'random' than sequences with conditional probabilities which are higher or lower.[3]

III. *Subjective Chance*

Passing now to the problem of subjective chances, the question in a nutshell is this: how many comparatively small chances do people tend to regard as subjectively equivalent to one comparatively large chance? Or, in other words, when is a multiple chance equated with a single chance?

This situation seems to be a paradigm of many circumstances in everyday and professional life when we have to weigh up several small contingencies and compare them with a single large contingency. Members of a jury may have to weigh several small probabilities of innocence against a single large probability of guilt (or vice versa). We can take another illustration from football. In the 1966 World Cup Games, far more attempts to score goals (by kicking) were made outside than inside the penalty area—563 as against 370—a ratio of 6 : 4. But only nine of the former by comparison with fifty-four of the latter were successful. From this we may infer that, in general, players prefer a larger number of attempts, each with a comparatively small chance of success, rather than a smaller number of attempts, each with a comparatively large chance of success.

The essential situation is simple. The subject is offered the possibility of winning a prize *either* by a single draw from an urn containing ten tickets where the probability of drawing the winning ticket is one in ten ($p = 0·1$) *or* by drawing a ticket several times from a second urn containing a hundred tickets, without replacement, where the probability of drawing the winning ticket, at the outset, is one in a hundred ($p = 0·01$). Let us refer to the first urn as A and to the second as B.

The results indicate that the modal indifference point, for 40 per cent of our subjects ($n = 150$, aged 17+), falls between nine and eleven draws from B, the urn with the larger number of tickets. (The 'modal indifference point' is defined as the number of draws in B at which the subject first changes his preference from A to B or vice versa). This leaves 60 per cent who either prefer fewer than nine or more than eleven draws from B to one draw from A. As we move from the mode towards fewer or more draws from B, the number of subjects having their indifference point at each value of x draws from B remains fairly constant.

The preferences for the single large chance, in relation to its mathematical advantage over the multiple chances, are plotted in Graph 1. From this it may be seen that as the number of small chances increases from one to eight, the preference for the single large chance declines from 97 to about 75 per cent. Between nine and eleven small chances, the preference for the single large chance declines from about 70 to about 30 per cent. And as the number of small chances increases from eleven to twenty or more, the preference for the single large chance diminishes to about 10 per cent or less.

Now if the preferences merely reflected the mathematical chances, they would fall, to the left of zero on the x-axis, on a line parallel to the base at the 100 per cent level. To the right of zero, they would fall on the x-axis. And at zero there would be a point at the 50 per cent

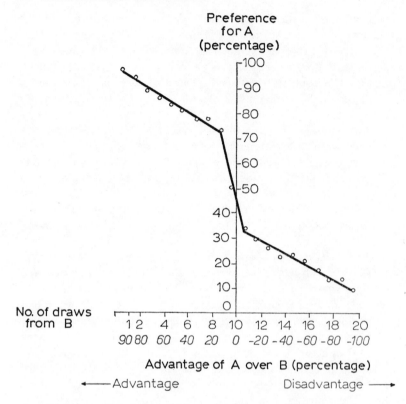

1. Preference for A in relation to advantage of A over B.

preference level. The gap between the observed preferences and this mathematical line may be taken as a measure of the divergence between psychological and mathematical chances.

Most of this divergence is attributable to the nature of the initial situation faced by the subject. If, at the start, the multiple chance is mathematically disadvantageous as compared with the single chance, a divergence appears when there are fewer than nine draws from B. Conversely, if at the start B is mathematically preferable to A, there is a divergence when there are more than eleven draws from B.

A second factor affecting the divergence is the size of the change in the number of draws from B in successive offers. The larger the step between successive offers of a multiple chance the more mathematically realistic are the preferences when there are less than ten draws from B, and the less realistic they are when there are more than ten draws from B. The order of presentation of the successive offers seems to have little effect on the choices.

By way of explanation it may be suggested that the 60 per cent, to which reference has been made, fall into two categories, the one overvaluing, the other undervaluing, the small chances, *as judged by their mathematical values.* Overvaluation occurs when the initial mathematical value of the small chances is relatively low; and undervaluation occurs when this initial value is relatively high.

This contrast is in accord with a phenomenon which we have repeatedly observed, namely, the tendency to overestimate an expected chance outcome, or an expected performance, if the chance is relatively small or if the task seems hard, and to underestimate it if the chance is relatively large or the task seems easy. Over- and underestimation are judged in terms of the mathematical chance or actual performance. In a range of experimental situations, estimates of performance appear to be most realistic when actual success occurs in about 30 per cent of the trials.

A word may be added in clarification of the two contrasting tendencies, overvaluing and undervaluing respectively. Several hypotheses present themselves which could be tested by further experiment.

(i) The overvaluers may believe that two chances are better than one regardless of magnitude *or* their scale of psychological probability might be such that even two mathematical small chances seem to them bigger than a single mathematical larger one.

Neither of these possible explanations could apply in the case of a choice between *one* small and *one* large chance. Here a preference for the former must, it may be supposed, be based on the greater thrill in drawing a winner from a hundred than from ten tickets.

(ii) The undervaluers may believe that it is all a question of luck, and therefore one chance is as good as twenty or more. This seems to happen in the British national lottery known as Premium Bonds. It might be expected that as the number of Bonds held increases from less than five to more than fifty there would be a corresponding increase in the proportion of Bond holders believing that they had a moderate chance of winning the largest prize. In fact the chance of winning this prize was felt to be best among those holding no more than six to ten Bonds. At this number, half of our sample[4] believed that they had a moderate chance of winning. When the number of Bonds held was less than six or more than ten, optimism was weaker. Furthermore three-quarters of the sample believed that a Bond holder would win a prize if he were lucky.

A second possibility is that the psychological probability scale of the undervaluers is such as to make a chance of one in a hundred seem less than one-tenth of a chance of one in ten. A third possibility might be that the manner in which the chances are mentally combined, in spite of their being correctly evaluated, reduces their impact. Finally, they may be seeking the option which carries the greater thrill.

Some of these factors came to light in a subsidiary experiment differing only in the fact that tickets from the urn with a hundred tickets were to be *replaced* after being drawn. Those who preferred a single draw even though it was mathematically *dis*advantageous, gave as a reason that the same non-winning ticket, in a multiple draw, might be repeatedly drawn.

A further question may be raised. What, if anything, are the subjects trying to maximize? The 40 per cent who make a realistic chance may be said to be maximizing the expected utility, but this cannot be said of the other 60 per cent. Those who overvalue cannot be said to be maximizing the mathematical probability, but they, or some of them, may be maximizing the psychological probability of drawing a winning ticket. In so far as their valuation of the prize is affected by their expectation of gaining it, they may also be maximizing their subjective utility.

Alternatively the overvaluers may be maximizing the thrill of play, in the sense that for them drawing two tickets twice is more exciting than drawing one ticket, while those who choose one small chance rather than one big chance may not be interested in multiple thrills but in a single large thrill.

The undervaluers are, to some extent, a mirror image of the overvaluers, while perhaps relying on luck. However, it is not necessarily a question of 'types of personality', because one and the same person may overvalue under some conditions and undervalue in others.

In conclusion, let me say that in so far as one can speak of an intuition of chance, one is not dealing with a simple contingency which is graded in magnitude and which has simple additive properties. The subjective magnitude of a chance (as in a lottery, for instance) seems inseparable from the number of such chances that are available to the individual concerned. I may perhaps add, in parenthesis, that people do not seem categorically to distinguish *chance* from *cause*. Possibly this is why their conception of an 'accident' as something that happens unexpectedly, unavoidably or unintentionally, bristles with contradictions.

IV. *Philosophical Considerations*

Perhaps the clearest philosophical position on the question of relation of chance to cause is the one taken by Hume.[5] He made an absolute distinction between them. The former, he says, is the antithesis of the latter. Chance is 'nothing in itself'; it is the negation of cause, and all chances are counted equal. The moment we allow one chance to be superior to another we introduce cause, on which is founded the principle of the inductive method based on the experience of uniformity. 'Chance', for Hume, has an equivocal relation to probability, which he regarded as being of two kinds: first, 'when the object is really in itself uncertain and to be determined by chance'; or when . . . 'tis uncertain to our judgement'. Possibly Hume did not regard chance as incompatible with determinism, at least in a statistical sense; an object which is 'really in itself uncertain' may yet be taken to mean 'statistically predictable'.

The distinction drawn by Hume was pressed further in the following century by Cournot,[6] who also admitted 'probability' in a double sense: first, with respect to the possibility of things independently of any knowledge that we may have of them; and secondly, in relation to our knowledge. He departed from the Laplacean view that chance is merely the expression of our ignorance (in which case 'le calcul des chances' would be merely 'un calcul des illusions'). He took the view that the calculus of chances is based on the combination or convergence of phenomena belonging to independent series, that is, parallel or successive series which are not causally interdependent. In this sense, he says, by way of example, that any relation between striking the ground with one's foot and a perturbation in the satellites of Jupiter would be pure chance. In other words, 'every event is causally connected with previous events belonging to its own series, but it cannot be modified by contact with events belonging to a different series'.[7] That is to say, a chance event, for Cournot, is 'a complex due to the concurrence in time or place of events belonging to causally independent series'.

The matter does not, however, rest there. Poincaré,[8] for one, was not content with Cournot's treatment of chance, but he seemed to waver between different interpretations. He began by assuming that naturally, as it were, the idea of chance expresses a state of mind. It is only 'a measure of our ignorance', in the Laplacean sense. But Poincaré, as Keynes remarks, immediately saw that this cannot be the whole story, for if a scientist discovers a law on Tuesday he would not then say that, on the previous day, the phenomenon governed by the law was nothing but a matter of chance. So Poincaré was disposed to include under chance (i) the effect of a minute cause that we cannot identify, for example, the birth of a genius; (ii) the effects of a vast number of causes which are too numerous to count, as in the molecules of a gas; and (iii) the coincidence of two distinct causal series (Cournot's case). Hence, to sum up, Poincaré in the end conceived of chance not so much as an expression of ignorance but as a positive assertion as to the manner in which the event in question comes to occur.

Keynes makes a shrewd comment on the ambiguity of the 'ignorance' of which chance is said, by Laplace and others, to be a measure. Ignorance as to the life expectation of individual clients is no barrier to the prosperity of an insurance company or to the receipt of dividends on the part of its shareholders. The ignorance is not absolute. An ignorance with respect to 'a' may not exclude useful knowledge with respect to 'b'. Keynes himself regarded 'objective' chance as a special case of 'subjective' chance, the former being applicable when an exact knowledge of fact, as distinct from principle, is needed for making even a rough estimate or prediction.

More recently A. J. Ayer[9] has attempted to distinguish five usages or meanings of chance:

(i) We speak of a chance event if it has an *a priori* mathematical probability of occurring. Thus we say that there is a one in eight chance that three successive tosses of a fair coin will all be head. (H.H.H. is simply one of the eight possible sequences). In this case, as is claimed in E.S.P. experiments, we consider that a deviation from the *a priori* is not attributable to chance. There is no implication that what is attributed to chance is uncaused.

(ii)   On the other hand, there are situations when we do attribute a deviation to chance, for example when a genetic mutation departs from a recorded frequency of occurrence. There is no contradiction with (i), however, because a recorded frequency is not the same as a set of mathematically equiprobable events.

(iii)   We say that an event occurs by chance when, so far as we know, no one intended it to happen. Such an event we think of as undesigned but not uncaused.

(iv)   We speak of the chance concurrence or coincidence of two events (Cournot's case). But if the concurrences are repeated, a point is reached at which we cease to attribute them to chance.

(v)   We assign to chance the determination of particular properties, for example, eye or hair colour in the children of a given family. (But this seems to me rather like an empirical analogue of (i) above.)

We cannot draw any factual conclusions from these philosophical reflections or analyses. If we wish to ascertain the facts we must pursue our psychological enquiries, which I now propose to do.

NOTES

1   Udny Yule, 'Notes on the Theory of Association of Attributes in Statistics', *Biometrika*, 1903, Vol. 2, pp. 121–34 (cited by Keynes, *A Treatise on Probability*, London: Macmillan, 1921, p. 165.

2   The first experiments in which these developmental trends were reported are described by J. Cohen and C. E. M. Hansel, 'The Idea of Independence', *Brit. J. Psychol.*, 1955, Vol. 46, pp. 178–90.

3   W. A. Wagenaar, 'Appreciation of Conditional Probabilities in Binary Sequences', *Acta Psychol.*, 1970, Vol. 34, pp. 348–56.

4   J. Cohen and P. Cooper, 'A Study of a National "Lottery": Premium Savings Bonds', *Occup. Psychol.*, 1960, Vol. 37, pp. 170–83.

5   D. Hume, *A Treatise of Human Nature* (Green's Edition), 1740, p. 424.

6   A. Cournot, *Exposition de la théorie des chances et des probabilités*, Paris, 1843.

7   Keynes, op. cit. p. 283.

8   H. Poincaré, *Calcul des probabilités,* Paris, 1912, 2nd ed., p. 2.

9   A. J. Ayer, 'Chance', *Sci. Amer.*, October 1965, pp. 45–54.

CHAPTER 3

The Chance of Success in Sequential Choice

I. *Introduction*

From single versus multiple chances in a lottery let us turn to the chance we believe we have in reaching an objective which depends on choices at a number of distinct stages. Imagine you are setting out on a journey which requires changing, say, six times along the route. At the outset, and at each stage or junction, you can choose between four different modes of transport, but only one of them will *certainly* succeed in catching the connection at the next stage; the other modes of travel would arrive too late. Unfortunately, you do not know which mode *is* the one you should take. Let us assume that you are indifferent as to these modes and that, so far as you know, they are all equally likely to be correct, how would you assess the chance of reaching your destination? More precisely, what betting odds would you equate with your chance of making the correct choice of mode at each and every stage? This situation exemplifies a common form of sequential choice, or 'decision chain', that occurs in everyday life as well as in industry, the professions and military affairs.

A rather special case is the prior prospect of achieving sainthood, when this depends on a sequence of more or less independent decisions. In the early history of canonization a simple decision was reached by popular vote or sentiment. In later centuries an interval of a century after death was deemed necessary to precede canonization. Like many other things, the procedure has now been formalized. In January 1971, Pope John XIII was reported to have passed the first stage, according to a document, signed by the Patriarch of Venice and prepared by a special court of enquiry.[1] But there is no time-table for the subsequent stages, at each of which unforseen doubts could arise. There might even be retrospective uncertainties which could annul a long-standing sainthood.

The general case is not limited to circumstances in which the choices must be made in a particular temporal sequence. There are multiple-stage predicaments in which the choices may be made either more or less simultaneously or in any order. Furthermore, the number of alternatives may vary from stage to stage, in which case the situation has a stochastic element.

The study of the manner in which people estimate probabilities has, in the past, largely been limited to situations defined by a single event, even if the event is repeated. Very little attention has been given to the manner in which they estimate a compound probability based on a sequence of events where the estimate may be subject to varying influences.

II. *Previous Experiments*

Our earlier investigations have shown that if a subject is presented with an $m \times n$ array of possible targets one of which is *the* unknown target, he does not treat the elements in the array as subjectively equiprobable targets. There are distinct preferences for locating the target in particular elements or zones. Some subjects seem to pit their wits against those of the experimenter in that they do not so much try to guess the location of a randomly placed target as to divine where the experimenter has actually placed it.

Our starting point was the observation that when subjects are presented with a page on which is printed a number of small circles (the number ranging from 2^2 to 2^{10}), and they are then asked to guess which circle the experimenter is thinking of, half of them choose a circle from the 20 per cent of the circles clustered near the middle of the page.

The same sort of thing happens when they are shown a square subdivided into $n \times n$ smaller and equal squares in one of which, the subject is told, a target has been, or will be, randomly placed.

These experimental situations differ from those commonly studied under the head of 'visual scanning' in which a signal is physically embedded in, say, visual noise—its size, illumination, frequency or scatter being systematically varied. I am here concerned with the task of *assigning* a signal to a particular location in a display; in other words, with an individual's expectation or confidence that a target will be, or has been, sited in a special part of a display. The problem here is thus one of preferentially structuring this display.

The results of seven experiments involving about 1,000 subjects, ranging in age from 14 to 23 years, who were given three choices, are shown below. In their first choice 60 per cent located the target in the upper left quadrant. There is a less marked preference for the upper half in the second choice, and for the lower half in the third choice. Only in one of the seven groups is there an apparent exception, the number of third choices in the lower half being slightly smaller than in the upper half.

TABLE 1   *Preferences by 972 subjects, for locations*
in three successive choices (percentages)

First choice		Second choice		Third choice		Combined choices	
60	17	30	29	11	25	34	24
10	13	22	19	32	32	21	21

If instead of presenting a set of squares we show a series of concentric circles, a similar effect occurs in that the different inter-circle zones are not felt to be equally likely locations for the target. It happens, however, that, in the case of circles, the top right quadrant is the most favoured first choice. It is possible that reading habits favour the response to a square display whereas aesthetic considerations are paramount in concentric circles, a hypothesis which could be tested. It is also conceivable that the apparent difference between the favoured location in the two displays conceals a common tendency to aim at the place where the display 'begins'. The circular display 'begins', as in a clock, near the number 'one'. The square display, as in a page, 'begins' where the text commences.

III.   *Sequential Choice*

From these experiments we may predict that in an $m \times n$ array with an unknown target in each of the m rows, the subject's estimate of his chance of guessing all targets correctly will tend to be exaggerated, as judged by the compound probability (n^{-m}) of locating the target. This prediction is supported by other evidence which indicates that when a choice has to be made at several stages, some people tend, in a curious fashion, to add, instead of multiply, the chances at the successive stages.

The experiments to be described are thus an exercise in subjective combinatorial analysis: given that the probability of gaining a prize depends on several independent probabilities, how does the subject combine them? Does he treat them as, in fact, independent, and, as it were, multiply them? Or does he fail to appreciate the multiplicative reasoning required and assess the chance of gaining a prize by some pseudo-additive operation? The procedure is as follows: the subject faces an $m \times n$ array, where m represents the number of rows or stages and n the number of columns or alternatives at each stage. At each stage there is one correct alternative. The subject's task is to select a lottery (from a set of fourteen lotteries) which represents what he believes to be his chance of guessing correctly at all stages (see Table 2). Only one guess is allowed at each stage.

Two independent experiments confirm the prediction. The experiments differed only with respect to the manner in which the subject

TABLE 2 *Lotteries as measures of* ψ

Lottery	Experiment 1			Experiment 2		
	No. of tickets	No. of winning tickets	p of winning	No. of tickets	No. of winning tickets	p of winning
1	100	90	0·9	11	10	0·91
2	100	80	0·8	12	10	0·83
3	100	70	0·7	14	10	0·71
4	100	60	0·6	16	10	0·63
5	100	50	0·5	20	10	0·50
6	100	40	0·4	25	10	0·40
7	100	30	0·3	33	10	0·30
8	100	20	0·2	50	10	0·20
9	100	10	0·1	100	10	0·10
10	100	1	0·01	1,000	10	0·01
11	500	1	0·002	5,000	10	0·002
12	1,000	1	0·001	10,000	10	0·001
13	5,000	1	0·0002	50,000	10	0·0002
14	10,000	1	0·0001	100,000	10	0·0001

estimated his chance of locating all targets correctly. In both cases his estimate was measured by his choice of one among fourteen lotteries, where the chance of winning ranged from 0·0001 to 0·9. The difference was this: in the one case, the total number of tickets was constant at 100 in ten of the lotteries, the number of winning tickets ranging from ninety to ten; and in the remaining four lotteries the total number of winning tickets was 500, 10^3, 5×10^3, and 10^4 respectively, with one winning ticket in each of these four lotteries. In the other case, the number of winning tickets was constant at ten in all fourteen lotteries, the total number of tickets varying so as to yield the same chance of winning throughout. The reason for examining the effects of the two lotteries is the fact that a losing ticket is not necessarily considered, subjectively, as the 'negation' of a winning ticket. Indeed it can be shown that lottery choices are systematically effected by the total number of tickets, as well as by the number and proportion of winning and losing tickets.

The subject's choice of lottery is regarded as his 'psychological probability' (ψ) of guessing correctly at every stage. In both experiments, which yield results which are virtually identical, all values of ψ are overestimates, as judged by the mathematical probability (p), thus confirming the prediction. But there is a differential effect in relation to columns (i.e. number of alternatives per stage) and rows (i.e. number of stages) respectively. The relation between the relative overestimation ($\log_{10}\psi/p$), and the amount of information in bits ($m \log_2 n$) required to locate the target, is linear (see Graph 2).

IV. *Inferences Drawn*

It is evident from these experiments that a clear idea of compound probability, even in its simplest form, is far from being primitive or intuitive. If so, this could help to explain why the subtlest thinkers of ancient Greece never came within reach of combinatorial analysis, although they, and particularly the Stoic philosophers, were much concerned with the idea of the possible, and they were familiar with the logic of disjunctive and compound propositions. Stoic determinism was able to reconcile a belief in the possible, due to ignorance of the future, with a belief in universal causality and the absence of chance. By contrast with Aristotle's extraordinary ingenuity in

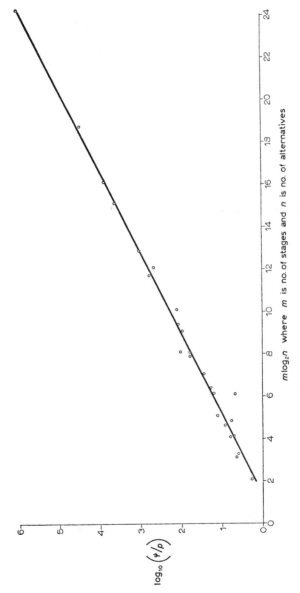

2. Log relative overestimation plotted against the number of bits.

other spheres of knowledge, his grasp of probability was elementary ('The probable is that which for the most part happens'),[2] though it is conceivable, as is implied by Sambursky,[3] that Aristotle's intuition of probability was enfeebled, as it were, by his strong belief in the differing causal systems in celestial and terrestrial affairs. Cicero, born three centuries later, flatly denied that if 400 dice were thrown, it would be possible 'by any chance in the world' for them all to come up sixes (*De Divinatione*, XIII). As is well known, the mathematician D'Alembert, in the eighteenth century, maintained that the probabilities of two successive throws of a dice are not independent. And he, as well as Buffon and Condorcet, attempted to draw a line between a bare possibility, which is below the threshold of probability, and a probability proper. A small probability (2^{-100}) is metaphysically possible, but physically impossible, said D'Alembert. Laplace[4], too, when he defined equally probable cases as those about which we are equally ignorant, seemed to treat the possible as a rudimentary form of, or as the limiting case of, the probable. Events are equally possible, he declared, when we are 'equally undecided about (them) in regard to their existence'.[5] But, as a thoroughgoing determinist, he should not admit the category of the possible, which is only, after all, a badge of ignorance. On the other hand, Boole,[6] took the view that 'the state of expectation which accompanies entire ignorance of an event is properly represented, not by the fraction 1/2, but by the indefinite form 0/0'.

In relation to criteria for establishing a scientific law, Borel[7] introduced a lower threshold for recognizing probabilities. On the cosmic plane, he declared, violation of the law is negligible when p is of the order 10^{-500}; it 'will never be observed'. On the terrestrial scale, $p = 10^{-15}$ can be ignored, and on the human scale, 10^{-6}. This is a prescription. The actual probabilities, transduced into their 'subjective' chances, which are ignored on the human scale, must be determined empirically. We can be sure that the observations would display complex patterns, varying with the individual and the situation.

We have elsewhere[8] discussed the subtle relation between 'the possible' and 'the probable', as well as the case for saying that the very notion of possibility entails probability. The inability to distinguish the two concepts is exemplified in football-pool punters who have a high degree of belief in the chance that they will win, undismayed by the fact that the odds against them are astronomically great. They seem to ignore the magnitude of the chance, and treat the mere *possibility* of winning as an appreciable *probability*. They either fail to co-ordinate two perspectives, or they treat the probable as a quantification of the possible.

We must accordingly reject the assertion that 'people are consistently conservative information processors, unable to extract from data anything like as much certainty as the data justify'.[9] The subjects we have studied 'extracted' far more 'certainty' than the data warranted. What seems to happen is that people 'extract' only a part of the information presented to them and their degree of certainty is unwarranted because it rests on only a fraction of the available information.

The problem of treating negligibly small probabilities, which exercised the minds of eighteenth-century French mathematicians, may have some rough analogue with the child's difficulty in coping with the idea of the very small. A child of 5 or 6 years of age can understand the idea of the infinitely or indefinitely large, but even a 7- or 8-year-old has difficulty with the idea of the infinitely small. This is how a 5-year-old defined 'infinite': 'It is a great enormous number even bigger than a trillion. It goes on and on and on and never stops'. But a 7- or 8-year-old soon arrives at a limit in struggling with the idea of 'infinitely small'. He thinks in terms of a minimum 'atomic' magnitude. He will say that a cake may be divisible into, say, twenty or thirty portions at most, but not into forty portions, for 'there would not be enough'. He adopts as his minimum a perceptible quantity. A smaller quantity, visible though it might be through a microscope, is not allowed; 'that would be cheating'.[10]

V. *A Related Problem*

A related problem of interest arises in respect to the manner in which uncertainty from two different sources blend, or are combined, in the mind of a given individual. We can examine three pairs of situations, viz:

(i) two sources of uncertainty, each relating to chance.

(ii) two sources of uncertainty, each relating to skill.

(iii) one source relating to chance and the other relating to skill.

In early adolescence two sources of uncertainty in one and the same situation yield larger psychological probabilities (= estimates of success) than would be expected on the basis of estimates made in two separate situations each with its own source of uncertainty. This is true whether the situation is chance-chance, skill-skill or chance-skill. This relative overestimation in a single situation is much more pronounced when both uncertainties relate to chance than when they relate to skill. The reason for this may be that in the former case subjects *add* or average two estimates, whereas in the latter they tend to *multiply* the probabilities.

A second effect is paradoxical in that, in certain circumstances, the psychological probabilities are larger when there are two uncertainties than when there is only one. This effect occurs when the probability attaching to the second uncertainty is greater than that attaching to the first, and the bigger the difference between the two, the greater is the paradoxical effect. On the whole, at this stage of development, a skill-chance situation is treated more like skill-skill than like skill-chance. When intellectual maturity is reached, at about age 20, there is more internal consistency. At this age, the psychological probability relating to two uncertainties in a single situation does not differ from the product of two separate probabilities each associated with a different situation.

However, returning to the main experiments described above, I wish to conclude with the suggestion that the hypothesis of an 'inertial-ψ effect' has been confirmed. There would thus appear to be a 'law' of sequential choice, such that if the number of stages in an array is held constant, the relative overestimation of the chance of guessing correctly at all stages varies directly with a power of the number of alternatives. If, on the other hand, the number of alternatives at each stage is held constant, the relative overestimation varies exponentially with the number of stages. The 'law' may apply to a wide spectrum of situations ranging from mountaineering, where the climber has to succeed at a number of distinct stages *en route* to the summit, to the planning of a complex business or industrial operation, like a Rolls-Royce engine.

APPENDIX 1

(In the second experiment the value -0.31 becomes -0.33).

In the first experiment the relation between relative overestimation and information gain is given by the equation:

(1) $\log_{10} \psi/p = 0.26m \log_2 n - 0.31$

(2) $\psi/p = e^{(0.86m \log_2 n - 0.72)}$

from which it follows that if the number of rows (= stages) is held constant ψ/p is directly proportional to a power of the number of alternatives per stage, whilst if the number of alternatives (= columns) is held constant, ψ/p varies exponentially with the number of stages.

From (2)

$$\psi = e^{-0.72} n^{-0.14m}$$

from which it is evident that the relative overestimation of ψ relative to p is chiefly attributable to a subjective attenuation of the multiplicative factor, m, an attenuation of about six-sevenths, within our experimental constraints.[11] The relative overestimation, designated 'inertial ψ' may be generalized to situations where the number of items per stage varies stochastically.

APPENDIX 2

It may be of historical as well as pedagogical interest to the reader to be reminded how Mary Everest Boole, the wife of George Boole, proposed, a century ago, to explain the idea of the infinite to young children. They are asked to imagine that there is a cake on the table in a given room, and they have to answer the question 'how many children can pass through the room and have a slice before the cake disappears?' This, she says, depends on two things: the size of the cake and size of each slice. If, for example, the cake weighs two pounds and each child's slice weighs two ounces, sixteen children can share the cake. Now this, like alternative suppositions about the size of the cake and the size of the slices, is tied to the hypothesis that each child does, in fact, have a slice. But suppose no cake is given to the children, how many can pass through the room before the cake is eaten up? The answer, she claims, is an 'infinite number'. 'Infinity', she says, means a discarded hypothesis, an escape from a rule, in this case, connected with the size of the cake. If no child receives any cake, the size of the cake then has nothing to do with the number of children who can get a share; 'infinity does not mean that there are enough children in the world now to go on passing through the room for ever'.

NOTES

1 The *Guardian*, 28 January 1971.
2 Aristotle, *Rhetoric*, i 2, 1357, a34.
3 S. Sambursky, 'On the Possible and Probable in Ancient Greece', *Osiris*, 1956, Vol. 12, pp. 35–48; *The Physical World of the Greeks*, London: Routledge & Kegan Paul, 1956, p. 179.
4 P. S. de Laplace, *Theorie analytique des probabilités*, 1847, 3rd ed.
5 *A Philosophical Essay on Probability* (trans. E. W. Truscott and F. L. Emory), New York, 1902.
6 G. Boole, 'On the Application of the Theory of Probabilities to the Question of Testimonies or Judgements', *Edin. Phil. Trans.*, 1857, Vol. XXI, pp. 597–652.
7 E. Borel, *Probabilities and Life* (trans. M. Baudin), New York: Dover, 1962, p. 28 (first published 1943).
8 J. Cohen and I. Christensen, *Information and Choice*, Edinburgh: Oliver & Boyd, 1970.
9 W. Edwards and A. Tversky, *Decision Making*, Harmondsworth: Penguin Books, 1967.
10 A participant at the Copenhagen symposium suggested, during the discussion, that the child arrives at an idea of the 'infinite' by successive addition, whereas he must proceed by successive divisions, a more difficult task, to arrive at an understanding of the infinitesimally small.
11 J. Cohen, E. I. Chesnick and D. Haran, 'Evaluation of Compound Probabilities in Sequential Choice', *Nature*, 1971, *232*, 414–6; and 'A Confirmation of the Inertial—ψ Effect in Sequential Choice and Decision', *Brit. J. Psychol.* (in press).

CHAPTER 4

Subjective Sampling and Inference

I. *Inference from Population to Sample*

From a discussion of independence and chance we are led to the part these ideas play in subjective sampling and inference. Let us begin by asking 'How does the information given to us about a population affect our judgement of a sample taken from it? One way of dealing with this question is to examine the subjective distributions formed from guessing the composition of samples drawn from a given population. To illustrate: suppose you are shown an urn and are told that it contains an unspecified number of beads each of which may be either blue or yellow. I am going to draw samples of beads from this urn and you are to guess their composition, that is, the number of blue and yellow beads in each sample. We shall consider three kinds of distribution formed by such samples, which we shall call Type I, Type II and Type III.

Type I. four beads at a time are drawn from the urn and placed individually in one of four beakers. You guess the colour of each bead, after which the beads are replaced. The procedure is repeated until we have sixteen sets of guesses, with four guesses in each set.

Type II. four beads at a time are drawn and are all placed in a beaker. This procedure is repeated until there are four beads in each of sixteen beakers. Now you guess the number of blue and yellow beads in each beaker.

Type III. The procedure is as in Type II, but you guess the number of beakers containing 0, 1, 2, 3 or 4 blue beads respectively, (or the guesses may relate to *yellow* beads).

The first feature that strikes us in the guesses that result from Type I procedure is that children (aged 10+) show a decided preference for symmetry, in the sense that the sixteen sets of four beads are frequently believed by them to be of the following kind, where B means blue and Y yellow.

BBBB, BYYB, BYBY, BBYY, YBBY, YBYB, or YYBB.

Much less frequent are asymmetrical arrangements such as BBBY, BBYB, BYBB, or YBBB (or reversing the B's and Y's). These asymmetrical arrangements are described by the children as ugly or unfair; hence they avoid them. We see here that, in their criteria for guessing, they employ an aesthetic judgement, which is at the same time an ethical judgement ('beauty is truth'). Their desire for equilibrium and equity evidently governs their interpretation of uncertain events.

Let us now pose a further question: what is the effect on the guessed arrangements of the sets of four beads if we tell the children in advance that the beads in the urn are in the proportion one blue to one yellow (i.e. 1 : 1)? The result is a marked increase in the number of arrangements believed to consist of two blue and two yellow beads. And if the children are told that the ratio of blue to yellow beads in the urn is 3 : 1, the effect is to increase the number of arrangements believed to consist of three blue and one yellow bead—an increase, that is, by comparison with the 1 : 1 condition. In the 3 : 1 condition, by comparison with 1 : 1, there is also an increase in the number of arrangements believed to consist of four blue and no yellow beads. In short, the conclusion we draw from giving some information as to the composition of the urn is that the children are thereby induced to regard each sub-set or sample of four beads as a miniature or microcosm of the population.

In Type II procedure, where the children have to guess the number of blue and yellow beads in each of the sixteen beakers, we find again that the children employ an implicit microcosm model. But here they do so in relation to the contents of each of the beakers. Thus under the condition 1 : 1 (where the children are told there are equal numbers of blue and yellow beads in the urn) they are much more likely to say that the number of beakers with four blue beads is the same as the number of beakers with four yellow beads, than they do under the condition 3 : 1. They also equate the number of beakers containing one blue and three yellow beads with the number containing three blue and one yellow much more often under 1 : 1 than under 3 : 1.

In Type III procedure, however, where the children have to guess how many of the sixteen beakers contain 0, 1, 2, 3 or 4 blue beads (or vice versa), the task is more difficult, and it is only when children have passed the age of 14 that, in general, their guesses are influenced by the information that the ratio of blue to yellow beads is 1 : 1 or 3 : 1 as the case may be.

From these experiments it is possible to identify four distinct stages in the 'intuitive' grasp of the idea of a binomial distribution Type III, between the ages of 10+ and 14+.

(i) the first stage is governed by a belief that the number of beakers containing 0, 1, 2, 3 or 4 blue (or yellow) beads will vary

(ii) at the second stage there is a distinct tendency to believe that more beakers (out of the sixteen) contain two blue and two yellow beads than any other arrangement

(iii) at the third stage, the belief emerges that the number of beakers containing one blue and three yellow beads is the same as the number containing one yellow and three blue. Likewise, the number containing no blue and four yellow is equated with the number containing no yellow and four blue

(iv) a fourth stage at which the number containing one blue and three yellow is believed to exceed the number containing no blue and four yellow (and similarly if the colours are reversed) is not yet reached at the age of 14+.[1]

The emergence of these stages cannot be attributed solely to the maturation of the intellectual powers without the influence of specific kinds of experience. In order to establish the comparative roles of maturation and experience, one would have to investigate children and adolescents in different cultures as well as in different social classes.

I might add that it would be interesting to enquire into the question whether this tendency to see the whole represented in the part has any analogue with ideas of the microcosm encountered elsewhere in the history of ideas. In ancient Greece a long tradition conceived of man as a microcosm of the universe or, more particularly, as constituted of the primal elements, earth, air, fire and water. This belief was perpetuated by the neo-Platonists, who regarded man as 'an abstract model of the world'.[2] In the monadology of Leibniz, the human soul reflects the world, like a mirror. Tibetan Buddhism and other cults held similar views. Hence the doctrine of humours, on the basis of the elements, as the essence of personality, from Hippocrates to Ben Jonson and modern endocrinology. In archaic thought there is a widespread belief in part-whole magic, and medieval alchemy was permeated with similar beliefs, which seem to be reflected in the doctrine of preformation in the history of biology. How pervasive in the mode of thinking of adults, we may ask, is this apparently deep-seated notion? Do we, for example, on seeing a Chinaman for the first time, endow him with all the qualities of inscrutability and mystery, which legend has built up in our minds as characterizing the Chinese as a whole? Do we see an individual Tory as an incarnation of Toryism and a Trade Unionist as an embodiment of Trade Unionism?

II. *Inference from Sample to Population*

I now turn to a third question: How do we make inferences from sample to population? To begin with, let us note that the drawing of inferences from samples is a basic feature of sense perception. When we scan, by eye or ear, when we taste or smell, we are trying to learn something about a population from the part of it to which we have access. Freud took the view that thought processes merely take this a step further. He described thought as 'an experimental method of dealing with small quantities of energy, just as a general moves miniature figures about over a map before setting his troops in motion'.[3] The 'groping forward' in thought, he says, 'was learned in sense perception',[4] and he repeatedly speaks of 'sampling' external stimuli or excitations from the external world. Whatever its limitations, this model has the virtue of drawing attention to the sampling character of certain forms of thought.

The experimental situation to be described may be introduced by reference to a scientist who used to chide his wife: 'My dear, you should never generalize, even from a sample of one.' Would he, we may wonder, have been content with a sample of two? and what faith would he have placed in generalizations based on it?

Suppose I have an urn with a population (n) of 100 beads. I tell you the number in the urn, and that each bead can be either blue or yellow. I draw one bead at a time from the urn, and show it to you, without replacing it. It is your task, after witnessing the drawing of what is for you the smallest sample, to guess or estimate the proportion of blue and yellow beads in the urn. Furthermore, you have to make your estimate at a pre-assigned level of confidence (ψ).

Given this procedure, it is possible to determine the smallest samples that are considered a sufficient basis for judging the composition of a population, at a specified level of confidence. The size of the population (n) may, of course, be varied within wide limits. Similarly, we can determine the smallest samples for judging a population of given size at varying levels of confidence.

Two identical experiments conducted with different groups yielded much the same results. If we compare the minimal sample required to estimate the composition of a population of 500 beads (in the ratio of six blue to four yellow) with the minimal sample required to estimate the composition of a population of 100 beads (same ratio), there is little difference, certainly nothing like the ratio of five to one in the two populations. Averaged over all levels of confidence, the mean increase in minimal sample associated with an increase in the population by a factor of 5, is of the order of 1·5. This fact is related to the stability of the composition of the sample drawn, one bead at a time, from the two populations. If the ratio of blue to yellow beads in the population had been different and, hence, yielded more fluctuation in the composition of the sample, it is likely that the minimal samples required would have been more closely related to the size of the population.

For the same reason, both when the population of beads was 500 and when it was 100, relatively small increases in the minimal sample were linked with large shifts in level of confidence in the composition of the population. With a population of 500 beads, the minimal sample only needed to be increased by a factor of 1·5 to justify an elevation of the level of confidence by a factor of 9; with a population of 100 beads the minimal sample increase was of the order of 2 when confidence was raised by a factor of 9. Clearly, the degree of stability in the composition of a sample is a very important factor in our judgement of the composition of the population from which the sample is drawn, and also in our level of confidence in this judgement.

Suppose now that the subject has made his estimate of the composition of the population on the basis of a sample, and we then increase the size of this sample, one bead at a time? How does he respond to this state of affairs? He could either allow the additional information to influence his estimate of the composition of the population, while leaving his confidence in his estimate unchanged, or he could retain his original estimate of the composition of the population and couple it with a different level of confidence. In fact, he prefers to retain his estimate of the composition of a population while changing the level of confidence he has attached to his estimate, rather than adhere to his level of confidence and alter his estimate. There is more inertia in the estimate than in the confidence. In so far as he changes his estimate, it tends to reflect the most recent additions to the sample drawn from the population. In so far as the level of confidence changes, irrespective of the estimate, it is apt to rise rather than fall.

These experiments may be described as a paradigm of a wide variety of situations in everyday life when we make inferences about a population from samples of limited size, the composition of which is beyond our control. The housewife purchasing apples in the light of the few she has tasted, like the politician formulating an immigration policy on the basis of the 'quality' of the immigrants already admitted into the country, is making inferences from a sample. An inference about the parent population may be associated with any degree of belief in its authenticity. By increasing the size of the sample, an individual, in theory, might prefer to adhere to the idea of the composition of the population he has already formed while altering his degree of belief or confidence, or he might allow his ideas about the composition of the population to follow the information revealed by the growing sample, but be inclined to remain at his earlier level of confidence. A person might, after seeing five Chinamen, say he is 'reasonably sure' that x per cent are Good and y per cent are Bad; after seeing half a million his percentages are now r and s per cent, but he may still be 'reasonably sure'.

More specifically, we could regard our experimental situation as a model, necessarily simplified, of the manner in which the results of a parliamentary election are announced. Let us assume that this is the *first* parliament, as in many African countries, and that the results of the voting are announced for each constituency in sequence. One could then compare the subjects' successive estimates of the ultimate composition of the parliament, with the corresponding computer estimates, based on clearly specified initial assumptions.

Such situations support the distinction between the 'probability' under discussion and that which is commonly called 'subjective probability'. The subject, as has been made clear, is not assessing a probability; he is estimating the composition of a population. Coupled with this, he is 'optionally stopping', that is, he is deciding, on the size of the smallest sample which would support his estimate, at a given level of confidence. Or, as the sample is increased, he estimates the composition of the population, at the same time stating his confidence in his estimate.

III. *Evidence, Contradicted and Uncontradicted*

We are now ready to consider a problem first raised a century ago by Alexander Bain, who argued that our degree of belief in a proposition depends on the extent to which we feel that it is contradicted by other evidence. Evidence which may be slight but uncontradicted, says Bain, impresses us more than massive evidence which includes even one contradictory element. 'The number of repetitions counts for little in the process, we are as much convinced after ten as after fifty. We are more convinced by ten unbroken than by fifty for and one against'. In putting this hypothesis to experimental test we find that not more than two-thirds of our subjects obey Bain's 'law'.. The rest disregard it. What is more, the majority are more impressed by ten against five (10 : 5) than by one against none (1 : 0).

Those followers of Bain, for whom 1 : 0 is more convincing than 10 : 5, state that, in order to reverse this relation, hundreds of additional items would be needed to support the ten and outweigh the five against. For these people, 1 : 0 is less convincing than $(10+x) : 5$, when $x > 300$. In other situations we find that 4 : 1 is more convincing than 2 : 0.

The evidential weight people attach to the exceptional item in a homogeneous series depends on its location in the series. It is felt to be more contradictory if it occurs towards the end than if it occurs elsewhere.

A question of particular interest in this connection has been raised by Edgar Morin,[5] apropos content analysis. Morin advocates what he calls 'structural analysis' rather than the conventional procedures of enumerating the frequency with which an item occurs in a text or film. What, for example, are we to make of the fact that 'Stalin' occurs ten times more frequently than 'Lenin'? By itself, mere repetition tells us little unless we take into account *what* is said each time. It is the *structure* of the whole that matters. A single or exceptional item or action may be far more significant than stereotyped repetition. Structural analysis proposes to do 'justice' to the rare or even the missing item, in opposition to that which occurs frequently. The choice of method—enumeration of items or examination of structure—will depend on our model of the situation, namely, whether we assume that all items or actions are to be given equal weight or whether the weight attached to each is to be determined by its role in the constellation of items as a whole.

IV. *Two Kinds of Evidence*

We can, it seems, distinguish two types of evidence—discrete and continuous. In the discrete type, the evidential weight attaching to any single item is unaffected by the weight attached to preceding items. In the continuous type, the evidence attributed to a series of items remains, as it were, in a state of suspended belief, until the series is complete. Thus one rude remark may retrospectively annul decades of amiable relations between two people. And you can never say of a man: 'He is a good motorist'. You can only say posthumously: 'He *was* a good motorist'. How would we assess a saint who at the end of his life commits a grave sin? We know that this is not uncommon in the early stages of a saintly career; the sowing of wild oats may even be an essential preliminary to eventual canonization. And, conversely, what is the condition of a man with a long record of vice who redeems himself by one significant good deed before he dies? Shakespeare, in a celebrated sonnet, shows that he was aware of the phenomenon, for he writes:

The painful warrior famouséd for fight
After a thousand victories once foil'd
Is from the book of honour razéd quite
And all the rest forgot for which he toil'd.

The reputations of politicians, like those of fighting men, may also be wrecked by one false move after many successes. In other situations this retrospective cancellation of evidence does not occur.

To sum up: So far, in this chapter I have been dealing with the subjective counterpart to statistical inference, with a view to determining the way, on the basis of samples varying in size and composition, we intuitively make inductive generalizations, with a given degree of belief, about the parent population.

V. *Critique of 'Trait' Theory*

The point at issue in the latter part of the previous section may be looked at rather differently and in a way that perhaps brings us somewhat closer to questions posed by quantum theory, which is bound up with the theme of the Copenhagen Symposium on Statistical Causality. Niels Bohr[6] has himself raised similar questions, which have been elaborated by D. Bohm; and Sir Cyril Burt has also devoted an important paper to this and kindred topics. Crude analogies between psychology and physics are suspect. In themselves they prove nothing, though they may possibly provoke a novel line of thought. The analogy I propose to draw seems, however, worthwhile contemplating, in so far as it is based on purely psychological considerations.

There are writers who treat human attributes or traits as intrinsic entities which are more or less immutable. Hence a technology of 'tests of personality' and inventories has been constructed which purports to 'measure' such attributes. I cannot enter here into the dubious logic of the idea of a 'test' as such, in the domain of psychology, or into the even more questionable belief that a complex, dynamical structure, like the human personality, can be 'measured' as one measures a man's height or weight. I should, nevertheless, like to raise doubts about the assumption, underlying the technology to which I have referred, namely, that the human environment, milieu or 'field' can be regarded as constant and as definable independently, *for psychological purposes*, of the individual who interacts with it. If this assumption is faulty, as it seems to me, we have to abandon the idea of intrinsic attributes with an immutable fixity, and replace them by properties which may undergo transformation even of the most extreme kind. A sinner may become a saint, and a saint a sinner. The hero may turn out, in certain circumstances, to be a coward, while the coward proves himself to be a hero. Gifted authors, like Anatole France (in his *Thaïs*) and Dostoevsky (in *The Brothers Karamazov* and other works) are well aware of these 'field' effects. Hence the poor predictive value of psychological assessments based on the doctrine of unchangeable traits, on which rests the faith of many technologists of personality. Much the same comment may be made with respect to the assessment of intellectual competence, given certain genetic boundary conditions.

Just as an electron has no intrinsic properties peculiar to itself alone but shares them with the systems with which, at different times, it interacts, so man may be said to lack intrinsic properties, in any absolute sense, since the attributes he displays are functions of his interactions with systems that evoke his diverse potentialities. Like an electron, too, a man is capable of undergoing a variety of transformations. And as an electron is identifiable by the way it reacts to electro-magnetic, mechanical or gravitational 'forces', so a man is identifiable by his mode of response to social and psychological influences and situations of various kinds. Only a man is several orders of complexity higher than an electron, in that the systems with which he interacts are not only, in one important sense, independent of him, they are also, in another but equally valid sense, dependent on him for the significance with which they are charged for him. Thus a telephone ring awakens a man in the middle of the night. It turns out the caller has dialled the wrong number, so that nothing in the life of the sleeper could have remotely caused the call. Nevertheless each sleeper would respond somewhat differently, according to the way in which he transduces the signal.

What I have said is not to be construed as an argument from physics to psychology. My aim is merely to draw attention to an analogue between two sets of phenomena, physical and psychological, the description of each of which may be valid in its own field. It remains to add that the foregoing psychological statements are not based on anything remotely like the evidence which could substantiate assertions made about physical events.

VI. *Psychology and Physics, a Further Link?*

Attempts are sometimes made to point to a possible application of quantum theory, particularly in its statistical aspects, to sensory phenomena. A century ago it was widely supposed that the human senses were crude instruments which a more benevolent Nature could have made far more discerning. It is a fact that only about one-seventieth of the entire electro-magnetic spectrum affects our vision, and if we could respond visually to infra-red, ultra-violet, cosmic and radio waves, we should be able to 'see' all sorts of things that are now invisible. And the same would be true if our auditory range were extended into higher and lower frequencies. But within the effective range, a limit has been reached, notwithstanding Coleridge who wrote, in 1817, that 'the delicious melodies of Purcell or Cimarosa might be disjointed stammerings to a hearer whose partition of time should be a thousand times subtler than ours just as the edge of a razor would become a saw to a finer visual sense'. He failed to realise that if our vision were more acute within its present range, the dimmest light would seem to us discontinuous; and if our ears were more sensitive, we should be much disturbed by the collision of molecules in the air. As it is, we respond visually, at threshold, to some six quanta of light energy. And the ear, in so far as one can make a meaningful comparison with the eye, is more sensitive still. At 300 cps 'we can hear a vibration of the air particles that is 100 times smaller than the diameter of the orbit travelled by an electron around the nucleus of a hydrogen molecule',[7] Hence thresholds of human sensitivity for sight and sound must be studied with statistical and probabilistic concepts similar to those employed in quantum mechanics.

We must, however, regard as doubtful the more specific analogy occasionally drawn between quantum and psychological theory with respect to brain and mind. Because the process of thought involves very small quantities of energy, it is therefore said to be subject to quantum-theoretical restrictions. Here, I fear, we are skating on very thin ice. It is true that the brain, with its 10^{10} elements, operates on something like 10 to 20 watts and, if used for heating, as Burt has remarked, would take three hours to boil a quarter of a litre of water. But it is a far cry from this fact to statements about quantum jumps in processes of thought. The brain's economical use of energy has little demonstrable bearing on the nature of thought, a word which covers a multitude of different operations. Individual differences in the rate of energy utilization by the brain seem to be incommensurate with corresponding mental differences; the brain of a Newton would not boil a kettle much more quickly than the brain of a mental defective. Moreover, the brain's utilization of energy is apparently much the same in sleep, and even in schizophrenia, as it is in normal waking consciousness. It seems, accordingly, a strain on language to try to relate the logical discontinuities (gaps, jumps) in the stream of conscious thought with quantal jumps in cerebral processes.

It may, indeed, be conceded that when a man tries to scrutinise his own thoughts he disrupts them in so doing. He is like a child who, in front of a mirror, peeps through his half-closed eyes to see what he looks like when he is asleep. In this respect, there is some resemblance to the interaction of the observer with his data at a micro-level in physics. But whatever validity might attach to a comparison between observer-data interaction in the two situations does not entail any necessary similarity between quantal processes in the brain and logical quanta in thought, which is what Bohm (op. cit.), admittedly as a sheer speculation, is proposing.

And finally, as to whether we can find, in the realm of psychology, any genuine instances of complementarity must remain, for the moment, open. Duality and 'supplementarity', and even dialectic, yes, but pairs of variables, the definition of each of which can only be made more precise by loss of precision in the definition of the other, these are hard to come by in psychology. Duality may be exemplified by speech and silence,[8] each being made intelligible by the other. Speech must be selective. If we said *everything* we should be understood no better than if we said *nothing*. A dialectical relation between speech and silence is beautifully exemplified by Kierkegaard from his own experience.[9] 'One gift has been given to me and in such a degree that I can call it genius—it is the gift of conversation, of being able to talk with everyone. This happy gift has been given to me to conceal the undoubted fact that I am the most silent man of my day. Silence hidden in silence is suspicious, arouses mistrust, it is as though one were to betray that one were keeping silence. But silence concealed by a decided talent for conversation—as true as ever I live—that is silence'. The same dialectical relation might be applied to clothes. 'Light hearted ladies' may be said to walk the street naked, but nobody knows because they are wearing clothes! Nakedness hidden in nakedness is suspicious, but when wrapped in clothes, could easily escape attention.

The wearing of clothes, or rather fashion, illustrates other dualities. First, in a woman's dress, the seductive appeal of what is revealed depends on what is concealed and vice versa. Secondly, the lady who sets the fashion abandons her unique mode when it is copied by the masses and becomes 'in fashion'. Thus the moment a dress is 'the fashion'. it ceases to be 'fashionable'. To be 'in fashion' is to be the more or less anonymous one among many, and it is the antithesis of 'fashionable' which signifies being distinctively unique. The decline of one depends on the rise of the other. In this sense there is a 'supplementarity', for each owes its existence to the other. But it is not the case that the measure of the one becomes more precise as the measure of the other becomes less precise. Hence we are not dealing with complementarity in its proper meaning.

NOTES

1 The experiments on which this section is based were conducted by C. E. M. Hansel and myself.
2 F. Bacon, *The Advancement of Learning*, II, x, 2.
3 S. Freud, *New Introductory Lectures on Psychoanalysis*, New York: Norton, 1933, p. 124.
4 Idem, 'The Mystic Writing Pad', *Collected Papers*, Hogarth Press and Institute of Psychoanalysis, 1950, Vol. V, pp. 175–80.
5 E. Morin, *New Trends in the Study of Mass Communications*, UNESCO, 1968, SCH/CS/158/5; see also O. Burgelin, 'Structural Analysis and Mass Communications', *Studies of Broadcasting*, Radio and TV Culture Research Institute, Nippon Hoso Kyokai, 1968, No. 6.
6 N. Bohr, *The Atomic Theory and the Description of Nature*, London: Cambridge University Press, 1934; D. Bohm, *Quantum Theory*, London:

Constable, 1960,; C. Burt, 'Quantum Theory and the Principle of Indeterminacy', *Brit. J. Stat. Psychol.*, 1958, Vol. XI, pp. 77–93.

7   G. von Békésy, Concerning the Pleasures of Observing, and the Mechanisms of the Inner Ear, Le Prix Nobel en 1961, Stockholm, 1962.

8   See Chapter 4 in the writer's *Homo Psychologicus*, London: Allen & Unwin, 1971.

9   S. Kierkegaard, *The Journals, 1834–54* (trans. A. Dru), London: Collins, 1958, p. 245.

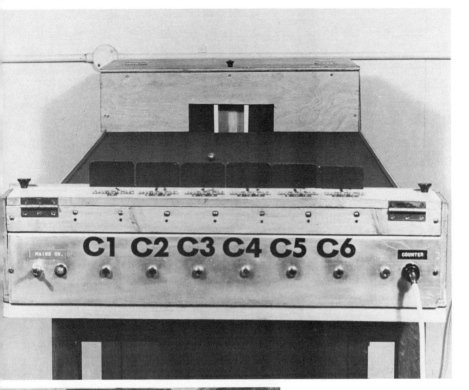

1. *Above:* The 'Tychotech' an apparatus for the study of preferences for different combinations of skill and chance (see Chap. 5, p. 3. *Left:* Van Mieris, 'The Doctor's Visit'—a representation of uncertainty in the minds of doctor and patient.

2. *Left:* Jean Arp, 'Rectangles Arranged According to the Laws of Chance', 1916. *Right:* Hans Haïm, 'Composing Music by Throw of Dice'.

CHAPTER 5

The Nature of Gambling

I. *Introduction*

The practice of gambling, age-old and world-wide, is not a topic that falls neatly within any single discipline. Its prehistory can be traced by the ethnologist, who compares the range and type of play in different societies. Its 'industrial' character engages the interest of the economist. Its quantifiable uncertainties excite the mathematical imagination; to problems posed by games of chance we owe the very existence of the theory of probability, with its reverberations ranging over the entire field of scientific effort. And while the ethical status of gaming belongs to the domain of the philosopher, the moralist[1] is not slow in condemning the vice and corruption with which it may become contaminated, leaving it to the politician to contain its usages within reasonable bounds. Psychologists should note, however, that the gambler himself is often deeply troubled by moral considerations. These, therefore, become the subject-matter of psychological science. While from each of these and other points of view we have something to learn: a proper understanding of gambling presupposes an ensemble of all the perspectives from which it might be viewed. Within this wider context, I shall dwell on motives and strategies, and on a distinction which I suggest is rather basic, between gambler and punter. Why do people gamble? What means do they variously employ to achieve their diverse goals? Why do only some become addictive?

I shall limit myself at the start to games of chance for financial gain, but later consider other situations. The so-called professional gambler will not be discussed for the simple reason that, strictly speaking, he is a business man, rather like the proprietor of a casino whose takings are more or less assured. Nor will I discuss the cheat, the 'percentage gambler' adept in swift calculation of the odds, or the expert at poker who bets only when he feels he has the edge over his opponent; these gentlemen deserve special treatment.

II. *Suggestions from Fiction*

It is convenient to begin by citing a famous work of autobiographical fiction which points to three characteristic and related elements in the mentality of a true gambler: first, his urge to enter into a contest; secondly, the significance for him of winning and losing; and thirdly, his supreme confidence, which he constantly must put to the test.

'At one moment', says Alexis Ivanovitch in Dostoevsky's *The Gambler*,[2] 'I must have had in my hands—gathered within five minutes—about 4,000 gülden. That, of course, was the proper moment for me to have departed, but there arose in me a strange sensation, the impulse to offer a challenge to fate, a wish to deal her a blow on the cheek, and to put out my tongue at her. Accordingly I set down the largest stake allowed by the rules—namely, 4,000 gülden—and lost.'

Here we have it, out of the horse's mouth. Dostoevsky, a man of consummate genius and inveterate gambler into the bargain, declares, in so many words, that the gambler is engaged in nothing less than a contest with Destiny. André Malraux's[3] gambler, Clappique, shares this engagement with Alexis Ivanovitch. 'This little (roulette) ball with its failing motion', he thinks to himself, 'was Fate itself—his *own* Fate moreover. He, Clappique, was contending not against a living thing, but against some sort of god: and at the same time, this god was his own self.'[4]

For this reason, the gain in itself, whatever its magnitude, does not satisfy the gambler. Nor is the largest permitted stake great enough. 'The gods' (the gambler may say to himself) 'have let me win £100. Will they allow me to win £1,000, £10,000, £100,000 . . . ?' There is no upper limit, for the wealth of the gods is inexhaustible, and no gain of a finite sum will convince the gambler that their coffers are open to him.

Nor does he want money for its own sake. Alexis Ivanovitch is perfectly well aware that he will only squander it 'upon some new Blanche and would spend another three weeks in Paris after buying a pair of horses which would have cost 16,000 francs'.

The gambler, therefore, if he is to persist in the face of repeated and crippling losses, must nourish an undying faith in ultimate victory. 'I am positive', declares Alexis Ivanovitch, 'that . . . I shall infallibly win . . . I only know that I *must* win.' He speaks as if (in the words of another gambler) he possesses an 'inner divining rod'. Yet, in spite of this assurance, he is 'obsessed with a desire to take risks'. He must always, that is, introduce an element of uncertainty in order to put his conviction to the test, like some St Anthony who conjures up tempting and delicious images only to prove that he can resist them. Alexis Ivanovitch speaks for all those gamblers who are dimly aware of a driving passion, but who know neither whence it comes nor whither it leads.

The autobiographical element in Dostoevsky's *The Gambler* is revealed by a letter he sent to his wife. 'I swear to you', he wrote, 'I swear to you it was not the love of winning alone, though I actually needed the money for the money's sake. . . . The gain of 4,000 francs destroyed me. The temptation of winning more (which appeared so easy) and in that way paying all my debts . . . it was too much for me, I could not resist it.'[5]

III. *The Question of Explanation*

Naturally, these citations from Dostoevsky do not amount to an *explanation* of gambling. Indeed the question: 'What constitutes an explanation of gambling?' admits of more than one answer. (The same is true, let me remark in passing, of all attempts at psychological explanation). We might be content with replies given by gamblers to the question: 'Why do you gamble?', but this would not be enough. The replies might be instructive, but we cannot assume that the information we seek is at the disposal of the gambler, and that he can reveal to us his deepest motives. Not that he would tell lies, or that his 'motives' are repressed (in the Freudian sense), but we cannot take it for granted that what is driving or pulling him is recorded in his word-store to which he has ready access. We cannot assume that the explanation for his conduct, in the sense of a description of its causes, is filed away in his mind or brain, awaiting retrieval. We have, therefore, to do the thinking for him, by making inferences about what lies behind his actions.

If, however, Dostoevsky's intuition could be verified, it might provide the basis for a theory of gambling, itself subject to further test. The question posed, accordingly, is this: Given that the gambler typically challenges Fate in the manner described, granted that his hope of victory at the gaming table is a mirage, that he plays to lose as well as to win, and that he must constantly submit his feeling of certainty to an ordeal, how does this pattern of ideas and impulses originate in the gambler's experience? To this question we shall later return. I need only add here the observation that the gambler's belief that he can foretell with absolute certainty the next event outcome in a game of chance, this belief which admits of no doubt, is perhaps only encountered at such a degree of strength in religious conviction and, in a coarser form, because largely based on self-interest, in political ideologies which thereby, possibly, betray their quasi-religious character. Somewhat removed from the politician is another godling, the judge, who pronounces judgement when the verdict seems to him or to the jury 'beyond reasonable doubt', a state of mind which has yet to be defined.

IV. *Gamblers Anonymous*

For obvious reasons it is not practicable to assemble a statistically representative sample of true gamblers. Nevertheless, a very rough approximation to such a sample may be found in the organization known as Gamblers Anonymous or GA,[6] which consists of erstwhile gamblers willing to seek assistance from it. Those members of GA that I have studied, all present a protracted history, often extending over two or three decades, of compulsive gambling. The sequence of events is monotonously uniform; casual gaming which grows into addiction; intermittent gains which blind the eye to frequent failure; financial ruin leading to borrowing and even theft; guilt, remorse, renunciation and then a relapse. Individual careers are pathetic or tragic, with economic collapse and domestic disruption. Members of GA realize that their affiliation to the group must endure if they are not to slip once more into their old ways. Whatever success GA may claim, it owes to the ritual of open and complete confession in an atmosphere of fellowship. Members feel that only they themselves can fully understand their common predicament.

What impresses us particularly in the study of Gamblers Anonymous is the austerity of gamblers. Contrary to popular opinion, compulsive gambling has nothing to do with sensual dissoluteness. While intent on his game, the gambler is oblivious of wine and women, and of the luxuries of the table. Hunger and thirst count for little with him, and his state of mind alternates between hope and despair.

GA flings its net widely but it still fails to catch the gambler who has drifted so far as to make his way of life irreversible, like patients suffering from a degenerative disease in its terminal stages. Even the gambler caught in the GA net cannot reveal the mysterious forces which drive him to his doom. But gamblers do agree on certain particulars evidently common to them all. Thus, money burns a hole in their pockets. When in possession of it they gamble it away or spend it in reckless abandon. There is nothing mean or parsimonious about them. Lavish and prodigal, they play the role of a tycoon and promise large sums when they do not have a penny to their name. At the same time, they nourish fantasies of grandeur, of becoming millionaires, of disbursing bounty and charity, and of establishing foundations and trusts; in their mind's eye they see themselves as princely patrons of art and science. There is something heroic about their readiness to part with money and the scale on which they do it. They hold cheaply what all others cherish as almost more precious than life itself. In this they stand apart from the rest of society. The most material of all values they seem able to regard with supreme contempt, a feat which one might expect the moralist to approve. On the one hand, their sovereign certainty of success enables them to hazard all they possess; on the other hand, what they possess they do not value, so for this reason, too, they easily part with it.

They are victims of a pathological compulsion. They resemble alcoholics who must drink ever larger quantities to yield the same effect as before. In the earlier stage of both addictions, the victim tries to prevent his craving from interfering with his work. In the later, pathological, stage his objective is to prevent his work, or what is left of it, from interfering with his craving.

V. *Gambler and Punter*

From what I have said, it seems to follow that we ought to distinguish sharply between the true gambler whose heart and soul are taken up with the game and the regular punter who stakes a comparatively small weekly sum on horses, dogs or football pools. The ordinary punter looks upon the prize as a desirable object not only before he has won it but afterwards as well. And he can stop his play whenever he wants to. The true gambler is different. He values the prize only *before* he has won it; *afterwards* it loses its attractiveness for him. The immediate gain is only a means to a goal which he can never achieve. So he cannot bring his play to a halt, and he tends to 'chase the winner' after each game; as his losses grow, so his hopes mount of winning in the end. But there is no end; no matter how much he wins he remains profoundly discontented. However high he climbs, summit after summit, there is a loftier peak to be scaled. The gambler persists in the face of all obstacles, and he can always brush aside any actual gain for another, imagined, gain of a higher order of magnitude. He is like a child who puts his parents' affection to trial: 'How far will they let me go?'.

If I am right in supposing that the utility of the gambler's prize changes its sign, as it were, from plus to minus, once it has been achieved, we may have here, in dramatic form, a basic tendency, widely shared, to devalue an object once it is within our grasp. A barrier between us and our goal, before it has been achieved, enhances its desirability. The mere fact that something is out of reach gives it an appeal. It is the hunt, not the capture, that matters. During wartime people form queues at shops even when they do not know why the queue is being formed. Something which is not in our possession we are eager to possess but once we possess it we are inclined to lose interest in it. Hence perhaps the antithesis between romantic love and marriage (see Chap. 8).

VI. *Models: Chance and Skill*

The experimental study of gambling is not directly concerned with the compulsive gambler, and it is doubtful whether one can extrapolate from such experiments to gambling proper in which real money is at stake. Nevertheless, the experiments may throw some light on the behaviour of the punter and they may even tell us something about the true gambler.

Experimental gambling has been mostly occupied with tests of a group of models which share in common two assumptions, viz:

(i) the worth of a gamble to a gambler is measured by taking the product of the utility of each possible outcome and its corresponding probability and then summing over all outcomes

(ii) the gambler chooses that gamble which yields the maximum sum of products of utility and probability.

The models differ mainly with respect to whether the utilities and the probabilities are to be measured on an objective or on a subjective scale. They take it for granted that gamblers, implicitly or explicitly, order the possible outcomes more or less logically and transitively, and then choose one, namely that which maximises the sum of products.

These models have been criticised on various grounds. In the first place, even when they do reckon with the player's psychological probability of success (ψ) rather than with the mathematical probability (p), they do not distinguish these from the element of subjective risk-taking on his part, in the sense of how sure he is that he will win. It is one thing for a player to assess the chance that a horse, a football team, or a group of numbers will win; it is quite another for him to have a given degree of assurance that he will be successful in betting on such a chance.

In the second place, the models often fail to acknowledge the part played by such factors as the variance of a bet; the effect of a belief in luck; the extent to which the gambler feels that the outcome depends on his skill rather than on chance or other factors beyond his control; the relative magnitudes of stake and prize; the utility of the gamble; interaction between the psychological probability of the gamble and its subjective utility; and the effect of continued play and practice.

If roulette players were 'rational', they would play in such a way as to maximize their gains. But they do not do so. Nor do they play safe so as to minimize their expected losses, which is not very surprising, for there would be little fun in gambling throughout a long session for the smallest gain and with the smallest chance of losing. They seem to enjoy the possibility of suffering large losses. In a recent study[7] of players at a casino, it was observed that a great number of gamblers preferred long odds and avoided bets which were almost fair. The assertion that 'gamblers do not like to lose (and that) they rather consistently prefer the alternative which leads to the lower probability of losing'[8] seems to fly in the face of the facts.

We can think of gambling situations as lying on a continuum such that, at one extreme, as in a lottery, the outcome is entirely outside the player's control and, so far as he is concerned, determined entirely by chance; and at the other extreme, as in chess, the outcome is, in principle, determined by the player's skill, though never completely so. Intermediate between these extremes, the outcome may be due to any particular combination of chance and skill.

What complicates the situation still further is that each player may attach different weights to the role of chance and skill respectively in determining the outcome. What seems to an authentic observer to be essentially a matter of chance may be regarded by the participant as governed by his skill. Thus those who habitually bet on horses and dogs, still less the bookmakers, do not look upon themselves as playing with chance to any considerable extent. Their self-image is that of assiduous students of form. They only place their bets after prudent deliberation, in the belief that they have selected the winning horse or dog on the basis of its superior capacity and other relevant considerations. Those who are attracted to horse- and dog-racing are disposed to draw a line between themselves and football-pool punters who (in their eyes) are true gamblers. And yet, many a football-pool punter, like many a roulette player, sees himself as engaged in a task solely requiring skill in seeking a predictable pattern of outcomes, though each outcome is, in fact, unpredictable.

Experiments suggest that there is a point on this chance-skill continuum, as subjectively interpreted, which, for any given person, appears to exert the greatest gambling appeal. On the whole, the more able prefer to gamble when the element of chance seems to them minimized and the element of skill maximized; the less able prefer situations in which these two components are ordered the other way round.

The experimental situation is presented as follows. The subject is first told that he has to propel a ball through an aperture such that he thinks he would succeed, at a given width indicated by him, *not more than* 2, 3, 4, 6, 8 or 12 times (according to the width) in twelve attempts. Let these six indicated widths be called sk_1, sk_2, sk_3, ..., sk_6, with psychological probabilities of success, 0·167, 0·250, 0·333, 0·500, 0·667 and 1·000 respectively.

The subject is now told that he will be given an opportunity to win a prize[9] by propelling a ball once through one of the apertures. He can secure a *playing* ball by drawing once from one of six receptacles each holding twelve balls and including, respectively, 12, 8, 6, 4, 3 or 2 playing balls. Let these be designated c_1, c_2, c_3, ..., c_6. The subject is allowed to choose one of the following six combinations in order to have a chance of winning a prize.

	^wsk	^wc	
sk_1	0·167	1·000	c_1
sk_2	0·250	0·667	c_2
sk_3	0·333	0·500	c_3
sk_4	0·500	0·333	c_4
sk_5	0·667	0·250	c_5
sk_6	1·000	0·167	c_6

It will be noted that the product of the two entries in each row is constant at one-sixth. The modal choice among the ablest subjects is sk_1 c_1, with sk_3 c_3 second in order of preference, and sk_4 c_4 and sk_5 c_5 almost totally neglected. Among less able groups (including teachers in training), the modal choice is sk_3 c_3. Illustration 1 shows a chance-skill apparatus, called *Tychotech*, devised to conduct these experiments.

VII. *Repeated Gambles*

A problem arises from this investigation. It will have been noted that the subject was given one opportunity only to win a prize. Let us suppose he is given repeated opportunities, and ask whether the choice of gamble is then influenced by previous play and, if so, in what manner. This question will be examined in a typical gambling situation.

By 'choice of gamble' in this context I mean, first, choice of the next outcome in a series of outcomes of a binary event; and, second, size of stake placed on the next outcome. In order to discover which gambling choices are made, we designed experiments in which students were given ten coins of equal value with which to engage in play. Each subject individually faced a roulette wheel, and he had to predict whether it would turn red or black. He could gamble *either* until he had run out of 'capital' *or* until he had made ten bets. If he guessed red or black correctly he won an amount equivalent to his stake. The maximum stake was a sum equal to his initial 'capital'. I shall confine myself to results obtained with forty-two adult subjects. Comparable, but not identical, experiments with younger subjects, aged 10+ and 14+ respectively, yielded similar results, but only a brief reference will be made to them because they raise other questions.

If we are to determine the effect of winning and losing respectively on a person's choice of outcome in his next bet we must compare the frequency with which he *changes* his chosen colour after he wins with the frequency with which he *repeats* the same colour after losing. If a player correctly guesses black, say, and predicts that red will appear on the next turn of the wheel, this means that he expects the wheel to alternate its colour at the next turn. But if he incorrectly guesses black, then, only if he again guesses black, do we infer that he expects the wheel to alternate its colour.

Table 3 shows the proportions of guesses and of individuals,

TABLE 3   *Effects of winning and losing on next guess*

Proportions of guesses, and of individuals,
(i) changing after a win, (ii) repeating
after a loss

$(N = 42, M+F)$

	Changing after a win	Repeating after a loss
Guesses	0·46	0·76
Individuals	0·48	0·87

changing their chosen colour after a win and repeating it after a loss. An individual is said to change his colour after a win if, after a win, he changes his guess more often than he repeats it; and similarly for repeating a loss.

In each row in Table 3, we can test the hypothesis that the proportions are approximately equal. Application of a suitable statistical test shows that, in both rows, the first proportion is significantly smaller than the second. From this we may deduce that winning and losing respectively at roulette have different effects on predicting the colour at the next turn of the wheel. After losing, there is a much stronger expectation that the wheel will turn to the other colour.

It does not follow that the *belief* that the wheel will turn to a different colour is stronger after a loss than after a win. On the contrary, there is some indication that this belief is actually stronger after a win. Thus if we compare the average stake placed in changing after a win with the overall stake placed in repeating after a loss, we find that the former is larger than the latter.

Let us now turn to the effect of winning and losing on the relative size of the next stake placed. We see from Table 4 that, for example, in seventy-six out of ninety-six bets after winning, the stake was larger than on the previous bet, whereas in only twenty of these bets was the stake smaller. After losing, however, the order of magnitude of the two corresponding figures is reversed. Thus the stake is more often increased after winning than after losing, although (in our particular experiment) about half of the stakes placed registered 'no change' either after winning or after losing.

TABLE 4   *Effects of winning and losing on next stake**

(N = 42, M+F)

	After a win		After a loss	
	Increase	Decrease	Increase	Decrease
Guesses	76	20	32	48
Individuals	25	1	13	19

*   Instances of 'no change' are omitted.

The same pattern of results appears if, instead of the size of the stake, we consider the number of monetary units added to, or subtracted from, the previous stake after winning and losing respectively. Again, we get the same result if we examine the data in terms of the number of individuals who increase or decrease their stakes after winning and losing respectively.

It may be remarked that the tendency of a gambler to increase his stake after winning is not a new phenomenon. As Xenophon[10] tells us, it was noticed in the fifth century BC by Calistratus, a popular orator, who observed, 'I cannot praise those gamesters who, if they are lucky in one trial, play for double stakes; for I see that the greater part of such adventurers sink into utter destitution'.

One further question: Do our roulette players prefer a strategy which is uniform or one which is variable? It seems that both types of strategy are equally favoured. That is, the numbers of players who change their choice of colour regardless of win or loss *together with* the number who repeat their choice of colour regardless of win or loss is roughly the same as the number of players who repeat their choice of colour after a win and change it after a loss *together with* the number who change the colour after a win and repeat it after a loss.

With respect to stakes placed, however, a variable strategy is generally favoured, viz. a tendency to increase the stake after winning and to decrease it after losing.

Finally, having regard to the three different age groups taking part in these experiments, let us ask what, if anything, they are seeking to maximize. The adult students and the youngest group (10+) are apparently trying to maximize, not their financial gain but the pleasure they derive from roulette. Judging by the stakes they successively place, they seem eager to prolong the experiment, as a game, as much as possible. By contrast, the middle group (14+) seem bent on minimizing their losses rather than on maximizing their gains. If so, our results are not in accord with the second assumption made by the models referred to above (p. 71).

VIII. *The Gambler's Fallacy and Negative Recency*

We are left with a theoretical issue. The difficulty which a number of investigators[11] have had in finding a relation between bets and stakes, on the one hand, and preceding gains and losses, on the other, is due,

I suspect, to a failure to distinguish two things, namely, the gambler's fallacy and negative recency. For this reason, it is often implied that losing and winning have similar effects on subsequent play. We have shown that this is not, in fact, the case.

It seems that there are at least three distinct situations:

(i)   the player knows the first k outcomes (red or black) and he has to guess the next one

(ii) he guesses each separate outcome in the series, each guess being followed (or not) by knowledge of results

(iii) he guesses *and* places a stake on the next outcome.

In the first of these three situations the individual's guess is only affected by his knowledge of previous outcomes. In the second, it is also influenced by his previous guesses, and by their accuracy or otherwise. In the third situation, something is at stake beyond the guess as such.

The expression 'negative recency' might be usefully kept for the first two situations, leaving the 'gambler's fallacy' for the third. The ground for this distinction lies in the apparent fact that the pattern of placement of stakes cannot be predicted from a knowledge of guesses previously made by a player. Whether a stake is raised or lowered does not depend merely on whether a guess has been correct or not.

The behaviour of our fictitious friend Alexis Ivanovitch illustrates the 'gambler's fallacy': 'After the sixteenth (or so) success of the red, one would think that the seventeenth coup would inevitably fall upon the black; wherefore novices would be apt to back the latter in the seventeenth round, and even to double or treble their stakes upon it—only, in the end, to lose.'[12]

But the matter is not so easily disposed of. Alexis Ivanovitch goes on to say: 'Yet some whim or other led me, on remarking that the red had come up consecutively for seven times, to attach myself to that colour . . . for I wanted to astonish the bystanders with the riskiness of my play' (loc. cit.). We thus also encounter a positive recency effect. And we note again the disposition to generate uncertainty both as a self-challenge and to impress the onlooker.

The gambler's fallacy reverberates in the hearts of us all, at least in the hearts of all those who subscribe to the dictum 'things must get worse before they get better'. In this respect, however, investors in British Premium Bonds are a race apart. For, as our investigations show, they refuse to believe that the longer their coupon has failed to win in the past the more likely it is to win a prize in the future. To make up for this loss of gambling spirit, they raise their eyes towards the future. Let no one imagine for a moment that the British national lottery is called Premium *Savings* Bonds by accident. For the moral worth of saving is a doctrine indefatigably preached by our theologically-minded politicians. Lord Keynes taught us that when men are selflessly thinking of nothing but their own gain, and save what they cannot spend, they are, by that act of austere renunciation, performing a supreme public service. No one, therefore, will wish to deny that the twentieth century is indebted to the inventive genius of Mr Harold Macmillan, a former British Prime Minister, for a twofold blessing. The Bonds which, in a moment of exaltation he conceived, enable us to achieve affluence in the flesh as well as salvation in the spirit by one and the same coupon. And the beatific mirage of everlasting glory is greatly enhanced by the minute chance of winning £100 *en route*.

I should like to refer to two further features of gambling at this point, which will be illustrated in later chapters. First, the fact that a gamble may be disguised by a temporal reversal of stake and prize (see p. 104). Secondly, generally speaking, the more remote in time the possibility of a gain or loss, the less credibility we attach to it (see p. 103).

IX.   *Gambling* With *and Gambling* For

The foregoing experiments exemplify gambling as a special kind of game played according to certain rules, as a more or less institutionalized, if deviant, activity, tolerated ambivalently though not totally suppressed. But both the motives for such games and the strategies that govern them enter into other forms of behaviour which, on the face of it, seem to have nothing to do with gambling. Any situation in which something is at stake in the hope of a larger, if uncertain reward, is, I would suggest, a gamble. We may therefore distinguish what a man gambles *with* and what he gambles *for*. The economist and politician are primarily concerned with situations in which both stake and prize are money; the interest of the psychologist extends to stakes and prizes of any kind, for there is no limit to the things one may gamble *with* or *for*, including health, reputation or life itself.

The illustrious physician, Asclepiades of Prusa, gambled with his reputation by making a wager with Fortune that he should not be deemed a healer if he were ever to become ill. He lost his life in old age by falling downstairs. Pliny[13] says he lost his bet, which seems to me an unfair judgement, for his death was not caused by illness.

The range of wagers in the records of gaming is a tribute to the amazing resourcefulness of the human mind. Eighteenth-century Britain distinguished itself in this respect. One man undertook to crawl on hands and knees all over England. Another was to chalk on every tree in St James's Park. A third, for a stake of fifty guineas, was to ride forty miles within three hours, drink three bottles of wine and untie the girdles of three girls.

Thomas Mann's widow, Hessenfeld, was not such a *rara avis* as her creator imagined. Her passion for betting led her to place every conceivable stake on the outcome of every conceivable event: 'the weather, the dishes at dinner, the result of the monthly examination, the prescribed length of stay of this or that person (at the sanatorium) the champions in skating, sleighing, bob-racing and skiing competitions, the duration of this or that *amour* among the guests, and a hundred other, often quite indifferent or trifling, subjects. She staked chocolate, champagne, and caviar . . . money, cinema tickets, or even kisses, given and received.'[14]

The difference between gambling *with* and gambling *for* is nowhere better illustrated than in Chekhov's tale *The Bet*. At a party given by a wealthy banker, the host enters into a dispute with one of his guests, a young lawyer of twenty-five, as to the relative merits of capital punishment and life imprisonment. The banker is convinced that life imprisonment is worse; the young man is equally convinced that any condition of life is better than death. 'Very well', says the banker, 'I am prepared to pay two million roubles if you remain in solitary confinement for five years'. 'I shall stay for fifteen years', replies the young man.

Thus the banker gambles *with* money, but the prize is an intellectual victory. The young man stakes his freedom, or rather renounces it for fifteen years, in the hope of gaining great wealth. In the event, the banker becomes impoverished, and just before the period expires plans to kill the young man so as not to have to pay the debt. He discovers the young man composing a letter stating that, having learnt to despise wealth, he is deliberately going to escape from his confinement some hours before the critical moment.

In the end, therefore, it turns out that the banker values his stake more than the demonstration of an idea; and conversely, the young man abandons the prize that lies within his grasp, because he has acquired a contempt for material things.

In de Maupassant's story *The Model*, financial gain enters neither into the stake nor into the prize. A young woman, for the sake of a passionate love, hazards everything on a single throw. Her lover is about to abandon her, and to prevent him she threatens to kill herself by jumping from a window. 'Do so, by all means', he replies, while graciously opening the window, not dreaming that she means to do what she says. She jumps. Shortly afterwards he marries her, though the fall has made her a wheel-chair cripple for life.

The most dramatic gamble is a gamble with life. The actual suicide casts away life itself in exchange for the possibility of something more precious, or less unpleasant. As to the so-called attempted suicides, most of these are anxious to live rather than to die, but with the advantages that would have accrued if they had in fact died. They want to have the cake and eat it. In attempted suicides, there are subjective as well as objective probabilities of dying. What the individual is doing is to stake some given probability (ψ) of dying for the greater probability of securing an advantage; if the probability of the latter is not subjectively any greater, it may be linked with a greater utility.

There seems to be a special affinity between suicide and gambling which rests on the fact that in suicide, too, there is, in a manner of speaking, a contest with the gods in the form of an ordeal. The attempted suicide is virtually saying to them: 'I am still alive: if you value my life and love me, you can still save me', just as the gambler could be saying, 'My losses are great, it is true, but you could let me win, if you approve my wishes.'

In a sense, gambling may be said to permeate our entire existence,

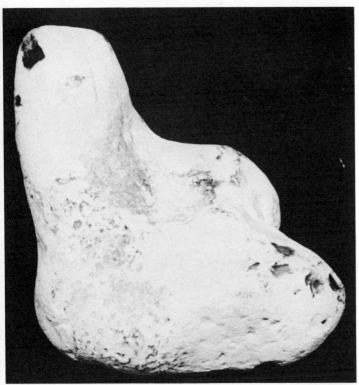

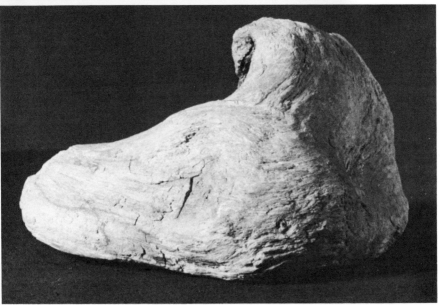

3. *Above:* A natural Henry Moore 'mother'-stone, formed by 'chance', and found by 'chance' on a deserted beach on a small island off the coast of Denmark. *Below:* Driftwood cast up from a lake after a storm: a natural 'work of art'.

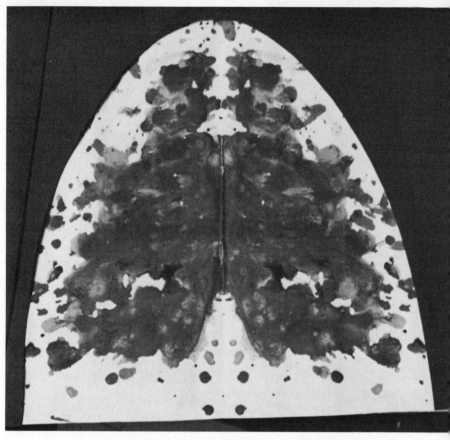

4. A face (or butterfly) formed by 'chance': a child pours paints on a page and folds the page.

for there are innumerable ways of hazarding something precious in the hope of gaining an advantage, in business, politics, love, sport, in driving an automobile, and in the act of self-destruction. Even an ecclesiastical career may be thought of as one in which certain earthly pleasures are staked, on long odds, for a more protracted celestial delight.

X. *Social Influences on Gambling Practices*

But when all is said, gambling is associated in people's minds with *financial* gain or loss. Financial gain is a prominent feature in the publicity employed by the successful proprietors of Nevada casinos. These proprietors know the bait which will catch the fish, and the promotion they employ taps the wish for quick, frequent and effortless gain, and the wish to economize (offers of free food and drink, free excursions etc.). But the desire for recreation is not ignored, and the atmosphere of the casino is a sporting one; opportunities are offered for golf, swimming, car-racing etc., and there are cabarets. Nor is the desire for social prestige disregarded: bets can be made on credit, and minimal stakes are high.[15]

The extent to which gambling flourishes in industrial societies seems to depend, among other things, on the gap between what punters want and what they can buy out of their earned income, their wants being powerfully and incessantly stimulated by advertizing. In communist countries, the state of affairs is not very different, for there, too, rare goods and services are only within the reach of those fortunate enough to win a prize in an official lottery. The gap is felt all the more keenly when economic success, as a rule, bears little demonstrable relation to merit. Gambling by the masses then becomes a means, if only in fantasy, of breaking out of their economic shackles. They know that a modest wage for daily toil will never bring them within reach of the things they dream of, and they are only reconciled to their drab existence by the hope that one day fortune may smile on them. In completing the fateful coupon, they cling to the possibility, which they treat as probability, that they can rise in the world and gratify their desires for material goals otherwise beyond their grasp.

So long as people crave for more than their resources allow, games of chance will continue to dangle their tantalizing appeal. And so long as a few will want to challenge the gods or, at any rate, test the degree to which they are ready to extend their favours, the gambler will remain among us and add his mite to the spice and misery of life.

XI.   *Calculating Systems*

Many a gambler is preoccupied with devising an infallible system to overcome the tricks of chance. But unless there is a mechanical or electronic flaw in the roulette or lottery wheel, his efforts are of no avail. For 'chance' obstinately refuses to submit to any system which will favour a given player. For this very reason, devices which depend on chance, like tossing a coin, have traditionally been used as a means of arriving at a just and impartial verdict. In such circumstances the 'gamble' is an appeal to divine justice. In football, for example, the two captains toss a coin to let the gods decide which side should kick off or which end to take. And occasionally, if a game is undecided after extra time, a verdict is obtained once more by tossing a coin. Italy 'defeated' Russia in this way at Naples in the 1968-9 Nations' Cup Series.

The disillusionment which a faith in gambling computing systems must inevitably entail can sometimes result in tragedy, such as befell a 56-year-old Englishman and his 45-year-old wife who, having lost their substantial wealth, attempted to recoup their losses in the French casinos. When their money ran out, they drove their car up a mountain track where they took their lives by carbon monoxide poisoning from the exhaust fumes. Their vehicle was well stocked with 'infallible' systems to beat the roulette wheel.

The same misguided faith appears in the tragic story of the Countess Lovelace, daughter of Lord Byron, immortalized in his *Child Harolde*—'Ada! sole daughter of my house and heart!' As a young girl of 15, Ada Byron was already displaying considerable mathematical prowess. Her teacher, the famous Professor Augustus de Morgan, described her talent as 'utterly out of the common way', and she was one of the very few people at the time who really understood what the celebrated Charles Babbage was doing when he built the first great modern computer. Her mathematical *Memoir* is the best available account of Babbage's stupendous Analytical Engine. Under the influence of her husband, the young Countess became a passionate devotee of horse-racing and betting, and constantly tried to exploit her knowledge of the theory of probability. The couple suffered very heavy losses which forced Lord Lovelace to renounce gaming, but the Countess secretly continued. Eventually she was reduced to pawning the family jewels, and she died from cancer at the age of 37.

XII. *Sex Differences in Gambling*

As a rule, in most societies, men have more and better opportunities for a wider range of gambling than women, and they also generally have more money to dispose of. This does not mean that the gambling impulse is absent in the fair sex. Given similar social and economic opportunities, little difference is to be expected. Ancient writers tell of fervent women gamblers. like Queen Parysates, mother of the younger Cyrus of Persia, and Ovid confesses that he would like his lady-love to know how to throw the dice skilfully, and to be able to calculate with precision the force she gives to the dice as she casts them.

During the eighteenth century when, in Britain, gambling practices reached unprecedented proportions, attention was frequently drawn to the increase of gaming in women. Sir Richard Steele deplored the effect of late hours and excitement on their appearance. 'The Beauties of the Face and Mind', he wrote, 'are generally destroyed by the same means. . . . Now there is nothing that wears out a fine Face like the Vigils of the Card Table, and those cutting passions that naturally attend them. Hollow eyes, haggard looks, and pale Complexions, are the natural Indications of a Female Gamester. Her Morning Sleeps are not able to repair her Midnight Watchings.'

Happily, today's Bingo sessions, whether in halls or in trains, do not burn the midnight oil, and it is Bingo rather than horse-racing or roulette that chiefly attracts the ladies, though they too are fond of trying their luck on football pools. As women gain equality in pay and other matters, they may confidently be expected also to challenge male supremacy in gambling.

XIII.   *Luck*

As we have seen above (p. 75), winning and losing do not appear to have the same effect on the choice of the next colour in roulette. There is an asymmetry in relation to winning and losing. Thus, while a player is winning, this very fact makes him feel that his 'luck battery' is being charged and that his good fortune will continue. So he continues to favour the same colour. And he may increase his stake more than if he had previously lost. On the other hand, while his opponent is winning, he may feel that his opponent's luck is being consumed while his own is being replenished, again as if his 'luck battery' were being recharged. However, this simple description does not exhaust the intricate yet coherent forms assumed by the belief in luck in shaping our conduct.

To a theologian, luck may appear as a secular species of divine grace. As such it enters as a term in the definition of hope for which we are indebted to Peter the Lombard (d. 1160) in *The Sentences*. It was given wider currency by Dante as 'the product of divine grace and merit preceding', a formula opposed by Luther. 'Merit preceding' may be regarded as an individual's self-assessment of past performance, which, when 'multiplied' by a belief in one's own luck, yields a measure of one's aspirations.

It was due to his belief in luck that Alexis Ivanovitch continued to play after his initial success. In doing so, he violated the first rule given to aspiring gamblers by the chairman of what was London's largest and most expensive gaming club (Crockford's), namely, 'Be perfectly clear in your own mind that there is all the difference in the world between luck and chance. Luck may give you an early and very good win. Chance will ensure that if you go on playing the tables, night after night, the wheel of fortune will turn, sometimes with disastrous results.'[16] Of course, from a statistical point of view, this distinction is not valid, but psychologically it makes sense if by 'luck' we understand an outcome, due to chance, which is favourable to the player. What the counsellor is saying is this: treat an early success as a chance event in your favour but do not expect chance to remain faithful to your interests.

I had occasion to refer earlier (as no more than a hypothesis to be tested) to the discrepancy which, in an industrial society, people may perceive between what they earn and its potential purchasing power. Yet, and paradoxically perhaps, they may be readier to accept inequality of incomes if they imagine that the Wheel of Fortune may suddenly turn in their favour. For a belief in luck has the effect of assuaging envy. Like a mascot, it averts the evil eye from those who prosper. People say of a successful man: 'He was lucky'. And it absolves those who fail from guilt for their failure: 'It was my bad luck'. On the other hand, we are apt, in our own minds, to attribute our success to skill, while the failure of others we readily ascribe to their ineptitude.

XIV. *Psychological and Ethnological Theories of Gambling*

Let me now return to my point of departure. In the idea that the gambler unwittingly throws down the gauntlet to Fate we are taken back to the obscure origins of gambling.[17] For man has a history as well as a nature, and in a sense, with certain reservations, his nature reveals itself in his history. We shall understand his nature better if we take note of his history, including his life history. This does not mean that we can identify psychological with historical explanation. To ask why an individual gambles is not the same as to ask how games of chance came into being thousands of years ago. Nevertheless the coincidence is impressive. The evidence suggests that games of chance began as a gradual secularization of divinatory rites,[18] a profane perpetuation of an act which had been a sacred confrontation of the gods, an act compelling, even 'blackmailing', them to reveal their secrets, especially secrets of the future. The art of divination was once well-nigh universal, and its influence immense—through the interpretation of natural omens and portents, through innumerable man-made devices, and through the ordeal, the riddle and the oath.

So natural did gambling seem to the ancients as a means of ascertaining their destiny that the gods themselves, in Nordic and Indian myths, were supposed to resolve their difficulties in this fashion. By casting lots, the universe was shared among the Greek gods. 'In the first place', Poseidon tells Iris, 'the lots being shaken, I was allotted to inhabit for ever the hoary sea, and Hades next obtained the pitchy darkness; but Zeus in the third place had allotted to him the wide heaven in the air and in the clouds.'[19] When Einstein remarked that 'der liebe Gott würfelt nicht' (our dear God does not cast dice) he was adumbrating an implicit model of a universe which could not be made intelligible as a vast statistical machine. Einstein forgot that many people have felt that such a model aptly fitted the facts.

The earliest games of chance are generally assumed to have been played with the astragalus (small ankle bone) of the sheep, goat or deer. Many astragali (perhaps too many) have been found on pre-historic sites, though we cannot be sure about the uses to which they were first put. The assumption that they were gambling implements is based on extrapolation from historical times. Egyptian tomb paintings show the astragalus in games with counters as early as the First Dynasty (c. 3500 BC). Dice excavated in Iraq and India have been traced to roughly the same period. At first they may have been two-valued, like the *vibhitaka*, a nut used for play in India in the Vedic period. The arrangement of opposite pips on a die summing to seven seems to have been known in Egypt about 1400 BC.[20]

To this day our playing cards are used at once for gaming and for telling fortunes. In Korea at the turn of the century, to take a well-attested instance, games retained their divinatory character together with their amusement value. Before the American Indians were herded by their white benefactors into reservations fit for bison, they were everywhere addicted to gambling in the form of religious practices. 'The gambler fasted, sought supernatural aid in dreams, observed continence, and burnt tobacco in honour of his *manitou*.'[21]

It is therefore not surprising to find that gambling is ubiquitous. If there is anything in common between the native Indians of North America and contemporary citizens of the US, between peoples of ancient Persia, Greece, Rome, India, China and the peoples of modern Europe, Russia and Latin America, it is their devotion to lotteries, dicing, card-playing, bingo, roulette or horse-racing. Everywhere people delight in the possibility of gaining, if not a huge fortune, at least a worthwhile prize. Largely impervious to variations in culture, gambling overrides religious, ethnic and ideological diversity.

Not that the national characteristics are entirely lacking. Spaniards, we are assured, become despondent when they lose. Italians put on a spurious gaiety, Frenchmen vent their disgust in execrations, Germans, after a *Donnerwetter* or two, return to their beer and 'ponderous cheerfulness', Russians smoke a little more nervously. Turks betray no emotion, while Englishmen lapse into a surly, brooding self-reproach.[22] Without taking such caricature too seriously, it may be said that fluctuations, such as they are, from country to country, from age to age, and from one sex or social group to another, are not capriciously inexplicable, but are demonstrably related to particular influences of an economic, social, cultural or political character. It is no accident, for example, that in Britain's hard-pressed economy, entire trains, suitably equipped, should be put at the disposal of British housewives for the sole purpose of permitting them to enjoy an entrancing journey while playing bingo, a joy enlivened by the occasional glimpse of a cow grazing in the countryside.

While the ethnologist seeks clues to the *social* history of gambling, the psychologist tries to make sense of the gambler's *individual* history, and hence of the fact that one man is content to stay a punter while another, gambling compulsively, marches inexorably to his doom. But just as the theory of divinatory origins, by inference from observation, attempts to reconstruct the past, so a theory of the ontogenesis of gambling derives, inferentially, the pattern of primal 'motivation' from the piecing together of behavioural facts.

The rudiments of such a theory we owe to psychoanalysis which does not, however, present anything like a coherent picture. For while sex inevitably makes its not entirely unexpected appearance, some analysts recognize that there is more to it than that. Freud took the lead.[23] Clearly, the gambler's conduct is inexplicable to us in terms of his conscious logic or sentiments, but it is nevertheless profoundly meaningful to him. It would not be difficult to write a gambler simulation programme for a computer such that, given a notional capital, the computer would follow a more or less consistent strategy which would end in utter ruin. But this would be a simulation exercise only by courtesy. It would tell us nothing about the *why* of gambling behaviour. We should be no wiser about the dynamical origins of the addiction in the gambler's life history.

A way out might be found by seeing the gambler's play as a symbolic representation. But what does it represent? In Dostoevsky's preoccupation with parricide, Freud claimed to find the key to his passion for play. He therefore suggested that the gambler is struggling to resolve, on a symbolic level, as in a dream, a conflict engendered by the so-called Oedipal situation in infancy. The gambler is enacting a pseudo-incestuous drama by posing two questions directed, as it were, to Destiny as a father-surrogate: 'Will my wish be potent enough to destroy my father?', 'Will I be pardoned (punished) for my guilty wish?'. His aim, unwittingly, is to compel his father to allow him to gratify his forbidden desires while protecting him from the consequences.

This conflict leads to a constant craving for paternal assurance, of which he can never get enough. If he is rejected, which means that he loses, his demands are intensified. And the heavier his losses, the more enslaved he becomes to the card pack or roulette wheel, in order not only to win but also to lose, so as to justify his raising the stakes and win yet more, while total triumph is forever beyond his outstretched fingers. Malraux hit the nail on the head (op. cit., p. 227). His gambler, Clappique, discovered 'the real inner significance of games of chance—the frantic fun of losing'.

The inference that a gambler wants to lose as well as to win seems less extraordinary when we recall that this is the case in all insurance. The man who insures his house against fire does not want his home to go up in flames. When he pays his premium he is encoding this message to the insurance company: 'I bet you £10 to your £10,000 that my house will burn down by the end of the year. If I win and it is destroyed, you pay me. If you win and it survives, you pay nothing. But I do not want to win.' A telling instance occurred in 1966. A Sicilian worker undertook to pay an annual premium of £18 to insure the virginity of his daughter for the sum of £575. She was setting out to work in Germany. We can be reasonably sure that he wanted her to return *virgo intacta* and that he therefore preferred to lose his bet rather than receive £575 if his daughter were to be deflowered.

The actual technique of play, Freud interpreted as a substitute for the compulsion to masturbate. In both, the hands are feverishly active; in both, the vow to renounce further play is invariably broken; in both, there is a vicious circle: tension, play, guilt and again tension followed by play; in both, it is a game for its own sake.

The ardour of gambling is accordingly an erotic ardour in disguise, a win signifying orgasm and a loss, castration.

And just as an oracular judgement is sought from the deity to permit masturbation without guilt, so the player compels Fate to allow him to gamble without losing. In both situations the higher powers are coerced into making a favourable decision.

Some slight support for the Freudian view may be found in the case-history of the gambler-patient who sought 'forgiveness' only when he lost, and in that of another who is said to have equated 'hitting the jackpot' with the experience of orgasm to which he also likened the 'stream of coins' flowing from the one-arm bandits; and in the teasing nature of play he saw himself asking: 'How far can I go without having an ejaculation?'[24]

All the same, even if we were to accept the theory of gambling as a symbolic incestuous drama, a number of obstinate difficulties remain. By what mode is one conflict transposed into the other? How does the gambler discover the isomorphism between the two patterns of experience? By what criterion does he decide that one fits the other? Such difficulties, it is true, face us in relation to any symbolic representation, but they cannot be brushed aside without jeopardizing the theory as a whole, which, in any event, is tenuous enough. Case-histories, moreover, are few and far between, and they do not carry much conviction. Nor, I have to add, either in unredeemed gamblers or in members of GA, have I been able to detect much hint of a symbolic scenario of incest.

Lastly, there is the puzzling question of the significance of winning and losing. How could Dostoevsky, in a letter to his wife, write that he had experienced an orgasm when suffering (enjoying) a *loss* at play? This suggests, in so far as it is allowed as evidence, that the gambler's aim is to lose as well as to win. It is therefore misleading as well as an over-simplification to assert, as some analysts do, that the gambler equates winning with orgasm and losing with castration. There is an obvious sense in which an orgasm is also a 'loss' and, at the same time, yields a thrill which generates guilt.

To the uninitiated, it must be admitted, the leap from the green baize table to the turbulent conjugal bed is a feat worthy of an intellectual kangaroo. A long jump of comparable dimensions was once made by Tristan from his own couch to the adulterous bed of

Isolde, so as to avoid leaving any footprints on the tell-tale ground. This Olympic leap was simultaneously a gamble, for Tristan surely staked his life for the sake of a few transient moments of carnal bliss. His gamble becomes intelligible only when we appreciate the high utility he attached to the payoff and his equally high psychological probability of success. He himself described the situation as a 'gamble for high stakes'. We must ascribe to him a large co-efficient of luck coupled with a generous self-estimate of earlier achievements.[25]

And now to sum up: a practice so ancient, so universal, so protean, so deep-seated and ineradicable, must draw its strength, not from an ephemeral or superficial whim, but from something fundamental in the human psyche, biologically perhaps as well as culturally. It is conceivable that a readiness to tolerate uncertainty was a selective factor in human evolution. And coupled with this, or perhaps an integral part of it, might have been the tendency for the common perils to seem less probable than the facts of life warranted; a tendency, that is, for hazard to exceed risk.

The ease with which men everywhere (and increasingly women too, and even children) become punters or gamblers, whatever the nature of stake or payoff, points, not to an instinct of gambling, but to a 'divine discontent' which is distinctively human. Animals do not play poker, nor are they interested in football pools. Yet they are capable of 'probability learning', and the fact that intermittent reinforcement renders their habits more resistant to extinction than continuous reinforcement suggests that arousal mechanisms may possibly be at work in a manner common to man and animal alike; an analogy between the self-stimulation of a rat with electrodes implanted in its hypothalamus and a man sitting in front of a one-arm bandit may not be entirely far-fetched.

There are signs, in the apparent convergence of ethnological and psychological theory, that some little light has been shed on gambling. Archaic divinatory practice was essentially a device for reducing uncertainty in decision-making. With the introduction of stake and prize more concretely, it was but a short step from here to the gamble proper. The invocation of supernatural aid in resolving uncertainty (explicit in divination) in gambling recedes into the background and becomes implicit. In the presence of agonizing, if non-conscious conflict, it is not so surprising if, by means of a gamble, the issue can be symbolically raised to a transcendental plane.

One thing seems evident. While we may all be inclined to devalue an object once it is within our grasp, the gambler displays this feature on a spectacular scale. The punter cannot be said to be greatly disillusioned when he wins. On the contrary, he clutches his gains tight to his breast, and the one thing he will not do is to imperil them in some hazardous enterprise. But this is, above all, precisely what the gambler feels impelled to do.

NOTES

1 The American moralist cannot complain of lack of fuel to feed the flames of his wrath. For on the heels of gambling, we are told, come 'the harlot, the pimp, the pick-pocket, the narcotics peddler, the safe-cracker, the stick-up-man, the blackmailer, the extortionist, the professional thief, the confidence man, the labour racketeer, the municipal fixer, the shakedown copper, the machine boss, the corrupt judge, and other paid protectors of crime, less easily condoned than gambling'. D. W. Maurer, 'The Argot of the Dice-Gambler', *Ann. Amer. Acad. Pol. Soc. Sci.*, 1950, Vol. 269. pp. 114–33.

2 The quotations from *The Gambler* are taken from the English Everyman edition, pp. 166, 298, 173 and 273, in that order.

3 In André Malraux's *Man's Estate* (trans. A. Macdonald), Harmondsworth: Penguin Books, 1961 (first published as *La Condition Humaine*, 1933).

4 Op. cit. p. 227

5 *Letters of Fyodor Michaelovitch Dostoevsky* (trans. Ethel Colburn Mayne), London: Chatto & Windus, 1914, pp. 113–4 and 119.

6 Like Alcoholics Anonymous (AA), which it resembles, GA has now spread to many countries. The apparent parallel between alcohol addiction and compulsive gambling, in respect to aetiology and 'psychodynamics' alike, would repay further study.

7 W. Edwards, 'Probability-Preferences in Gambling', *Amr. J. Psychol.*, 1953, Vol. 66, pp. 349–64.

8 B. Hochauer, 'Decision-Making in Roulette', *Acta Psychol.*, 1970, Vol. 34, pp. 357–66.

9 Alternatively, he may be told that this is a new form of Russian roulette; he will lose his life if he chooses a playing ball and propels it through the aperture. See J. Cohen and C. E. M. Hansel, 'Preferences for Different Combinations of Chance and Skill in Gambling, *Nature*, 1959, Vol. 183, pp. 841–2.

10 Xenophon, *Hellenica*, VI, 3.

11 W. Edwards, 'Subjective Probabilities Influenced from Decisions,' *Psychol. Rev.*, 1962, Vol. 69, pp. 109–35; M. Greenberg and B. Weiner, 'Effects of Reinforcement History upon Risk-Taking Behaviour', *J. Exp. Psychol.*, 1966, Vol. 71, pp. 587–92.

12   *The Gambler*, p. 273.
13   *Nat. Hist.*, Vol. VII, p. 37.
14   Thomas Mann, *The Magic Mountain* (trans. H. T. Lowe-Porter), London: Secker & Warburg, 1946, p. 296 (first English edition 1928).
15   H. F. Hess and J. V. Diller, 'Motivation for Gambling as Revealed in the Marketing Methods of the Legitimate Gambling Industry', *Perceptual and Motor Reports*, 1969, Vol. 25, pp. 19–27.
16   Mr Tim Holland in *The New London Spy* (ed. H. Davis), London: Blond, 1966, p. 157.
17   Possibility of some interest in this connection is the spontaneous expression of related ideas. On 12 May 1966, *New Society* reported a double 'seismic' shock in the US. One was a drop in Wall Street shares after General Motors had announced short time for their workers. The other was China's detonation of a nuclear device. An insurance official at Lloyds commented 'What I'm doing is playing dice with God'.
18   E. B. Tyler, *Primitive Culture*, New York: Harper, 1958 (first published 1871), Vol. I, pp. 78–83.
19   *Iliad*, XV
20   E. N. David, 'Studies in the History of Probability and Statistics', *Biometrika*, 1955, Vol. 42, pp. 1–15.
21   S. Culin, *Korean Games, with Notes on the Corresponding Games of China and Japan*, Philadelphia: University of Pennsylvania Press, 1895; see also H. Lüders, *Das Würfelspiel im alten Indien*, Berlin, 1907, and H. J. R. Murray, *A History of Board-Games, other than Chess*, London: Oxford University Press, 1952.
22   A. Steinmetz, *The Gaming Table*, London, 1970, pp. 212–3.
23   S. Freud, 'Dostoevsky and Parricide', *Collected Works*, Vol. 5, pp. 222–42, London: Hogarth Press, 1950 (first published 1929).
24   R. M. Lindner, 'The Psychodynamics of Gambling', *Ann. Amer. Acad. Pol. Soc. Sci.*, 1950, Vol. 269, pp. 93–107.
25   *Tristran of Gottfried of Strassbourg* (trans. A. T. Hatto), Harmondsworth: Penguin Books, 1960, Chap. 23.

CHAPTER 6

Uncertainty in Medicine

I. *Sources of Uncertainty*

'Medicine is a science of uncertainty and an art of probability.' Few doctors will deny that there is some substance in Osler's dictum.[1] But what is the precise nature of the uncertainty and probability to which he refers? This is the topic to which I turn in this chapter.

It will help, to start off with, if we distinguish two categories of uncertainty, which may be called intrinsic and extrinsic respectively. Intrinsic uncertainties are those pertaining to the imprecision, ambiguity or other limitation of the data on which a medical judgement is to be based. The determination of a blood cell count is a good example. This will vary from one patient to another, and one and the same patient will not necessarily yield the same count from one day to the next. Inter- and intra-patient variation will be increased by differences in the size of the (blood) sample taken, in the technique of sampling or in the instruments employed.

Extrinsic uncertainties, often misleadingly called 'observer error', make their appearance in the interpretations given to a set of data. Here the interpretation may vary from one assessor to another, while one and the same assessor may, on a second occasion, give an interpretation which differs from the one he gave on the first. Inter- and intra-assessor variation may even apply to the sounds transmitted by a stethoscope. The growing literature on 'observer error' in roentgenogram diagnosis and cancer cytology has recently been reviewed by Lusted (see note. 1.) He points out that experienced assessors of chest roentgenograms may fail to recognize about 30 per cent of films showing positive evidence of disease, while 2 per cent of negative films are treated by them as positive. Moreover, inter-assessor disagreement occurs in about one-third of the instances, and inconsistency on the part of one observer in about 20 per cent.

In considering inter-assessor variation, special attention should be paid to the fact that the medical novice not only notes less than the experienced clinician, but his judgement is less precise. His physical examination of a patient, like his case history, will be a procedure which follows the text-book in a more or less routine fashion, whereas the specialist will intuitively take 'heuristic' short-cuts, and move more rapidly to what seems to him, and to what probably will be, a correct diagnosis.

In arriving at a diagnosis, conditional probabilities [$\psi(D/S)$] generally play a part, and these probabilities are psychological. Given S, a pattern of symptoms, ψ, the conditional psychological probability of a certain disease, D, will vary from one doctor to another. And conversely, there will be a corresponding variation in the inferences drawn from disease to symptoms. Given a certain disease, the conditional psychological probability that the patient will present a particular pattern of symptoms [$\psi(S/D)$], will vary from doctor to doctor.

In current attempts to computerize diagnosis, an effort is made to replace subjective considerations by recorded frequencies and other data. The question remains, however, whether, and to what extent, a computerised system can simulate the intuitive assessments of an experienced clinician. This question is part of a wider issue, namely, whether it will be possible to render the creative processes of the human mind in a formal language intelligible to a computer. I am inclined to doubt whether the model, advocated by Lusted, of the diagnostic process as a decision tree or net with nodes as testing points for hypotheses, does justice to the complexities of the situation. This model fails to take account of the 'search' character of diagnostic procedures.

A doctor's uncertainties may also relate to the treatment he proposes to give. Should he, for instance, advise a dose of Testosterone for impotence or is such therapy contra-indicated because of possible drug dependence or side effects? Sometimes it is possible, in principle at least, to measure his state of mind with some precision. Suppose he is in doubt as to whether his treatment will be effective, we can say to him, following a suggestion made by Borel (see p. 26): You can choose between these two possibilities:

(i) *Either* you receive a sizeable reward if your treatment is successful

(ii) *Or* you will receive the same reward if a tossed coin turns up head.

If the doctor assesses the chance that the treatment will be effective as greater than 50 per cent, he will choose option (i), and he will choose option (ii) if he thinks the treatment has less than 50 per cent chance of being a success. If he chooses option (ii), we can then offer him either option (i) or option (iii), which is an event with a probability of 49 per cent; for instance, choosing a red card from a pack of one hundred cards consisting of forty-nine red and fifty-one black. If he prefers option (iii) to (i), we can proceed to option (iv), which has a probability of 48 per cent, and so on, until he prefers option (i). We infer that his psychological probability lies between the last two successive alternatives to option (i).

It would be wholly impracticable to eliminate all uncertainty, intrinsic and extrinsic. Risks must be taken and hazards must be incurred, if advances in therapy are to continue. But risks and hazards can be minimized.

Not only what a man is suffering from, or how he should be treated, is subject to uncertainty, but also whether he is alive or dead. This problem has been posed sharply in relation to decisions on heart donors. In 1968, when Britain's first heart transplant took place, the cardiologist took the view that in deciding whether a man is dead or not 'we must weigh up the evidence'—in other words, assess the probabilities; while the transplant surgeon argued in favour of the need for establishing multiple criteria of death, in view of the uncertainties associated with any single one.[2]

II. *Meaning and Credibility of Medical Pronouncements*

If a doctor allows his private uncertainties about diagnosis or therapy to be guessed by his patient, the latter may impose his own construction upon them. For the patient as well as the doctor is subject to uncertainty of varying kinds and of varying degrees. In a man who discovers that he is a victim of cancer, writes Professor Hinton, 'all the normal assumptions about the future and all the usual plans and hopes can suddenly dissolve into *uncertainty* (my italics) . . . he hopes that luck has not deserted him.'[3]

Consider the state of mind of a person who is in doubt about the meaning of the following pronouncement, or about its applicability to *him*: 'Present statistics indicate that more than 50 per cent of all cancer patients could be cured if the disease were diagnosed in its earlier stages and if prompt and appropriate treatment were given.'

This WHO statement[4] is presumably intended to encourage those who suspect that they may be victims of cancer to seek early medical advice. But its precise interpretation is open to doubt. How valid, some may wonder, are 'present statistics'? When do the 'earlier stages' terminate? Who would include himself in the 'more than 50 per cent'? What is the time-scale of 'prompt'? And how can 'appropriate' treatment be guaranteed?

Thus the meaning given to a typical medical message at its source is not necessarily identical with the meaning read into it at its destination. And even if the meaning of a message were unequivocal, there would remain the question of how credible it is. The credibility of a message may be assumed to vary with the knowledgeability and trustworthiness attributed to it, as well as with its content and form. Its content may be threatening or humorous, and its form may be slogan-like or flexible and adapted to varying circumstances. We must look to future research, however, to decide whether, for example, a graphic display of diseased lungs acts as a deterrent to smoking in proportion to its horrific quality.

A message may be perfectly credible as well as unequivocal and yet remain ineffective. Millions of smokers who accept the evidence of a causal relation between cigarette smoking and cancer, nevertheless manage to persuade themselves that the evidence does not apply to *them*. Many medical students reject the evidence of a link between cigarette smoking and lung cancer on the ground that evidence is 'only statistical'.[5] Many motorists, too, although perfectly familiar with the broad facts of road accidents, are convinced that road hazards do not concern them.

We have also to bear in mind the point raised at the beginning of

Chapter 1 which is relevant here: the sheer *amount* of information transmitted to a patient in a message from a medical source is not necessarily the same as the *amount* registered by the patient. It is safe to infer that much medical advice directed to the public never reaches its destination.

III. *Deciding to Seek Advice: A Model*

What influences a patient's decision to seek early medical advice? There are two main factors. First, there is the degree of doubt he entertains about his health; and secondly, there is the degree of seriousness he attaches to the possible illness. The former may be regarded as his psychological probability of illness, and the latter as the disutility he assigns to it. Psychological probability may here be measured on a scale from zero to 1, where zero signifies complete absence of doubt about health and 1 signifies subjective certainty of illness. Disutility ranges from one extreme, which the individual feels to be minimally unfavourable, to the other, which he feels to be maximally unfavourable. These two variables are not mutually independent. They interact in various ways. Four main types of interaction are schematically represented in Graph 3, where psychological probability is the dependent, and disutility the independent, variable.

The first type, $(a_1 a_2)$ may be described as an optimist, for he thinks that the more serious an illness, the less likely it is that he will suffer from it. The second, $(b_1 b_2)$, is the pessimist, who reverses this line of reasoning. The third, $(b_1 a_2)$ is sceptical about the possibility that he will be afflicted by a very mild or a very serious illness; while the fourth $(a_1 b_2)$, conversely, thinks extreme possibilities are more likely to happen to him.

These four types are not necessarily represented in the population with equal frequency. The first type may, indeed, be the commonest, as embodied in the belief that cancer always attacks *other* people. However, a pure type is a statistical artefact. Most people are 'mixed' types.

We can invert the relation of psychological probability and disutility and treat the former as the *independent*, and the latter as the *dependent* variable. Statistically, of course, the probability of

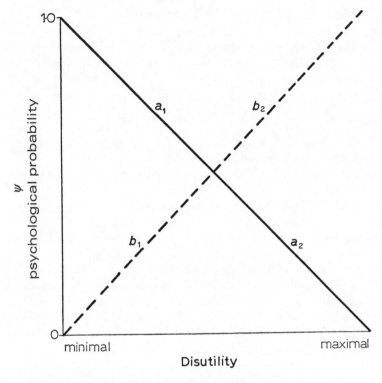

3.   Relation of psychological probability of illness to its
     subjective disutility, (adapted from Slovic, 1966).

illness is independent of its seriousness. But subjectively there is an
interaction such that, for instance, people may react to a rare event
as if it were comparatively common simply because if it *did* occur,
the consequences would be disastrous. Thus, an ex-commando of
World War II refuses to travel by air, knowing that casualties are
exceedingly rare, because if a crash did occur it would probably be
fatal.
   The pervasive belief in luck affects our judgement here as in
gambling. If a man thinks he is unlucky, he will unwittingly inflate
what he thinks is the probability of a serious illness, as judged by the
'true' probability, and vice versa, if he believes he is lucky.

IV. *Interpretation of Chance in a Medical Context*

When a person is considering the possibility or the probability of his being ill, his mode of reasoning, such as it is, commonly involves the idea of 'chance'. Imagine someone is told that, if he smokes x cigarettes daily for y years, he will have a 50 per cent chance of dying from lung cancer before age z. Does he understand by this '50 per cent chance' that his fate will be decided, as it were, by a toss of a coin? If so, this would be a depressing error on his part, for the '50 per cent', properly speaking, refers, not to the fate of an individual, but to groups precisely defined and distributed in a specified manner with respect to the probability of the death of their members at any given age. If, on the other hand, he treats the expression '50 per cent' as conveying maximum uncertainty, he would again be misled, for the message asserts a 'positive' probability.

This last point merits closer attention. Many people interpret statistical frequencies as if they were measures of subjective uncertainty. Take this example. People in England have been informed that 13 per cent of the population lose all their teeth before they reach the age of 21. A typical individual may reason as follows: this means that one in every eight persons, on the average, will lose all his teeth before reaching the age of 21. Therefore, in every group of eight persons, on the average, we can be certain that one of them will lose his teeth; in a group of seven persons, we can be 91 per cent certain; in a group of six persons, 78 per cent certain; in a group of five persons, 65 per cent certain, and so on until we reach *one* person, in which case we can be 13 per cent certain that he will lose all his teeth before reaching the age of 21. Such reasoning transforms a statement about the frequency in a population into a numerical statement of degree of certainty with respect to each individual member of this population.

The calculation is, of course, erroneous. In a group of eight the probability that none of them will lose his teeth is 0.87^8, i.e. $(1 - 0.13)^8$. Hence the probability that at least one of them will lose his teeth is $1 - (0.87)^8$. And the probability that in a group of seven, at least one will lose his teeth, is $1 - (0.87)^7$, and so on. But even if the calculation were correct there would still be a question as to the legitimacy of the use of a calculus of frequency as a basis for a measure of belief in the individual case.

A related but perhaps less controversial problem was posed fifty years ago by F. P. Ramsey.[7] Consider a number, *n*, of identical occasions in a proportion, *m*, of which a given proposition is true. Is a belief, of degree *m/n*, most appropriate to such a proposition? Ramsey seemed to think that the answer is 'Yes', and he took the view that there is a sense in which a statement of frequency and an expression of partial belief are the objective and subjective aspects of 'the same inner meaning'.

This amalgam of relative frequency and degree of belief was suggested, in the seventeenth century, by Locke,[8] himself influenced by the *Port Royal Logic* (1662). Probability for him is the agreement or disagreement between two ideas by proofs which do not have a constant and immutable connection with another, but only, *for the most part*, 'enough to induce the mind to judge the proposition to be true or false'. This state of mind Locke calls 'belief' (assent or opinion). Recognizing, further, that there are degrees of belief or assent, Locke distinguishes two sorts of proposition which we accept 'upon inducements of probability'. One concerns matter of fact and is subject to the evidence of our senses (i.e. what we should perhaps now call 'perceptive'); the other concerns things which are beyond the testimony of the senses. The first is exemplified by a rule in English law, namely, that though the attested copy of a record is good proof, this is not true of a copy of a copy, however well attested it may be. The second (beyond sensory testimony) is illustrated by the manner in which Nature works. 'We see animals are generated, nourished, and move; the loadstone draws iron; and the parts of a candle, successively melting, turn into flame, and give us both light and heat. These and like effects we see and know: but the causes that operate, and the manner they are produced in, we can only guess and probably conjecture. *Analogy* in these matters is the only help we have. . . .'[9]

My dental example relates to the interpretation of a statement about frequency in general. If an individual is *himself* involved in a grave predicament, his reasoning may take a different form. If he is told that nineteen out of twenty people recover from the illness of which he is the victim, he may think that he is destined or pre-destined to be the unfortunate twentieth. Conversely, if he is told that nineteen out of twenty die, he may think that he will be the one to survive. An interesting case arises, in the latter circumstance, if the surgeon confides to his patient that nineteen out of twenty die, that he has already operated on nineteen, and that they all died. The surgeon, arguing from the false principle of negative recency, may feel that the twentieth patient must survive, while the patient, reasoning from positive recency, is convinced that he is doomed.

In point of fact, these sanguine and lugubrious interpretations respectively are only two members of a larger class of interactions between the psychological probability of an outcome and its subjective utility. There are other ways in which each of these, as a dependent variable, may vary with the other as an independent variable.

It is also common for people to employ actuarial thinking in situations where it is not applicable at all, and where only 'idiographic' considerations are relevant, that is, those which pertain to the unique pattern of experiences and events that characterizes a particular person. If the relapse rate in a disease, under given conditions, is x per cent, it does not follow that each patient has an x per cent chance of relapsing, regardless of the course of action he takes. Each patient either will or will not relapse. Prediction with respect to individuals is unjustified where the data only provide a basis for prediction with respect to groups. Doctors could profitably devote some attention to their use of the notion of 'chance', for this is a complex idea which enters into diagnostic and therapeutic procedures as well as into the patient's hopes and forebodings.

V. *Thresholds of Information, Belief and Action*

A doctor must have a minimum degree of belief in his diagnosis to justify his use of a particular therapy. The potential patient, similarly, requires a minimum degree of belief that he has lapsed from health before he will seek treatment. In both cases there are three distinct thresholds.

(i)   First, there is the *information* threshold. What is the minimum information each requires to know about the situation?

(ii)   Second, given the requisite information, there is the *psychological probability* threshold. How sure does each have to feel about the hazard to health?

(iii)   Third, there is the *action* threshold. Granted that information is adequate and that the hazard is appreciated, what inertia has to be overcome before action is taken?

So far as health education is concerned it is not enough to provide the public with relevant information as to the causes of disease or its likelihood. For individuals will differ in their information, probability, and action thresholds. Some will be more information-hungry than others. When all are sufficiently informed, some will be convinced more readily than others. And when all are convinced, some will act sooner than others.

It cannot be assumed that, in every case, the more 'weighty' the decision the more information the individual will require before making it. The decisions of kidney donors illustrate this dramatically. A study of some thirty donors or potential donors revealed that most of them made an immediate commitment, often by telephone, before enquiring into the possible consequences. They were prepared to undergo the operation long before the renal transplantation team had conducted the necessary tests to determine their medical suitability (blood compatibility etc.). Fourteen out of twenty donors and five prospective donors awaiting the operation stated that they had decided 'in a split second' or 'instantaneously'. A similar *immediate* decision was made by those who had been approached and refused to act as donors.[10]

Hence 'knowing' something is not an adequate basis for taking responsible action. We are reminded of the McNaghten Rules in legal psychiatry. According to these rules, laid down in Britain in 1843 (and later adopted in the US), a person is not to be held responsible for a crime if, when he committed it, because his mind was diseased, he did not know the nature of the act, or, if he did know its nature, did not know that it was wrong. Both Socrates and Confucius equated virtue with knowledge. Yet modern psychological science teaches us that there is a sense in which one can 'know' something while this knowledge has no impact on our sense of the rightness or wrongness of a given action: and even when this 'knowledge' is accompanied by a clear sense of good and evil, an individual's action may not necessarily be governed by it. A man may do something the nature of which he clearly understands is contrary to what he regards as right or wrong.

The question of thresholds may be illustrated by reference to the fluoridation campaign in the US, the relative ineffectiveness of which has been variously explained.[11] Many people were said to be either ignorant of the facts or they regarded the possible advantages of fluoridation as too indirect and complex to be worth bothering about. Hence, these did not cross the *first* threshold. Others, who doubted whether dental decay was a serious threat to health, had not crossed the *second* threshold. Nor had those crossed the second threshold who denied that an individual as such could do anything about fluoridation and insisted that it was a matter for socio-political action. This last view carried its own dangers. For when a referendum was, in fact, resorted to, it allowed excessive play to the 'lunatic fringe' opponents of fluoridation, as well as to those who opposed it 'on principle', or on the ground that it was harmful.

One conclusion from the study of the fluoridation campaign bears on the first threshold noted above. The case for fluoridation was presented in an excessively 'rational' and factual form, with insufficient appeal to emotion and sentiment. If so, it would seem to follow that the idea of an 'information threshold' must be amplified to include emotional as well as cognitive information. People have to be persuaded, not only educated. They must have their feelings stirred as well as be fed with facts and figures, for many people reject or ignore medical advice which runs counter to their favoured habits.

VI. *Effect of Time in Relation to Illness*

A special factor must be singled out for emphasis, because of its effect on the way someone may treat the possibility of illness. I refer to the temporal factor, namely, the period of time which a person believes must elapse before illness will make its presence felt. His subjective estimate of this period of time affects his response to symptoms of incipient malaise. So the decision he makes about his mode of living, or about his diet, will depend on when, in his view, he will feel the effects of this decision. Other things being equal, the more remote in time the effect, whether it be favourable or unfavourable, the less it will shape his immediate decision.

Remoteness in time not only enfeebles the subjective utility or disutility of the outcome of one's decision, it also weakens the expectation (psychological probability) of its occurrence. The issue arises pointedly in relation to smoking. What is the effect on a teenager who is told that 'the man of fifty smoking twenty or more cigarettes a day has double the chance of dying in the next ten years than the non-smoker'? The prospect of 'dying' after four or five decades is not very terrifying to a young person, while to be told that he will have 'double the chance' of dying when he is 55 years of age is to rob death of its sting.

It is this remoteness, or apparent remoteness, in time of the effect of smoking which may explain why so many smokers cross the information and hazard thresholds but not the action threshold. The prospect, for a 20-year-old person, of a year snipped off his life half a century ahead, is not very alarming. It might be a much more potent deterrent to impose a penalty of 'dying' for an hour immediately after smoking a packet of cigarettes.[12]

The element of time, by a reversal in the temporal order of stake and prize, helps to disguise the gambling character of smoking. In the typical case we hazard a shilling for the chance, say, of winning a £100 next week. In smoking a cigarette, we hazard the health of our lungs in the future for the sake of a pleasant sensation in the moment. The gamble is hidden because the reward is immediate and certain, whereas the fate of the stake belongs to an apparently far-off day to come. The smoker secures a significant utility *now* in exchange for the disutility of a possible curtailment of life decades ahead.

VII. *Mental Epidemiology*

I have so far been dealing with the manner in which incomplete, vague or uncertain information is assimilated by individual persons. But the diffusion of ideas and practices relating to health and disease also depends on factors of a social character. Their spread in the population is not random but follows an identifiable course. An epidemiological model has accordingly been suggested[13] to represent the observed phenomena. On this model, the dissemination of a given belief or habit (craze, cult, fashion, etc.) follows the pattern of physical epidemics. At the start there is a latent period during which the idea or practice, though beginning to 'catch on', does not show much sign of spreading. During the second phase there is a relatively rapid diffusion, sometimes an explosive one. In the third phase, the susceptible population becomes saturated, and the velocity of the wave, so to speak, loses its impetus. A fourth phase follows during which resistance to the practice grows, rather like the growth of immunity to physical infection; there is a waning of enthusiasm in those already mentally infected. Finally, at the fifth phase, if the belief or practice still survives, it is static, and perhaps cultivated only by a small number of ardent people.

The rise and decline of fashion in medical and surgical therapy are phenomena which can be verified by the history of medicine, though a quantitative measure of the changing effect over time is not easily devised. Voltaire, in *The Child of Nature* (1767), speaks of the doctors of his day who confounded the disease of the patient they had seen last with that of the one they were to see next, and who made the evil twice as great as it had been before by their haste 'in prescribing some remedy which happened then to be in fashion. Fashion even in Medicine! That folly was only too common in Paris.' Sometimes, as in the thalidomide affair in our own day, the spread of a drug can be arrested with dramatic abruptness, but usually the decline is gradual.

The use of thallium therapy in the treatment of diseases of the skin illustrates the point at issue. Between 1914, when this type of therapy was first mooted, and about 1925, there appears to have been little active interest in it, as judged by the *Index Medicus*. This, then, was the first or latent period. Between 1926 and 1928, the second phase, there was apparently a rapid rise in the popularity of thallium. Thousands of patients were treated all over the world. The third phase—the period of gradual decline—began about 1929 and continued until about 1934. Subsequently, during the fourth phase, 'immunity' started to set in, as judged by the proportion of papers drawing attention to the hazards of thallium therapy. The final, quiescent, stage was reached about 1940, when interest in the subject seems to have all but died out. We have used this epidemiological model to study the growth of medical and other scientific societies in Britain from the eighteenth to the mid-twentieth centuries.[14]

VIII. General Conclusions

Many a decision about health and sickness is made, and action taken, in a kind of twilight of uncertainty or incomplete knowledge. Or, because of uncertainty or incomplete knowledge, neither decision nor action is taken. This applies both to doctors and to patients. How are statistical pronouncements interpreted by them? How are the information-gaps filled? What distortions enter in their respective evaluations, and how does a belief in the seriousness of a disease affect one's belief in the likelihood of its occurrence? In particular, there is the more general question of messages, transmitted under tacit but unjustified assumptions about their meaning.

Investigation suggests that individuals, according to age, sex, individual background and other influences, vary in the manner in which they treat messages about health or safety conveyed to them through different channels. It cannot be taken for granted that the intended meaning of a message is uniformly received by those to whom the message is directed.

The effectiveness of health education depends, among other things, on an understanding of the manner in which people interpret information concerning their health about which they have some degree of uncertainty. It is one thing to compose a 'health message', it is quite another thing to ensure that it is grasped in the same sense by those for whom it is designed; and to grasp it is, again, not the same thing as to act upon it.

I have discussed the manner in which doctor and the potential patient interpret their uncertainties in relation to health and sickness. The proper interpretation of these uncertainties is essential for effective doctor-patient communication. It is worthy of note that, in spite of the great advances in medical science, 'fringe' medicine flourishes even in countries (such as Britain) which provide a National Health Service. Rational and irrational medical practices can evidently coexist in the same culture, and even in the mind of one and the same individual. Hence the cult of astrology, still very much alive, and fostered by the press in many developed countries, tends to keep alive the medieval belief that medicine is merely a branch of astrology.

To counteract these retrograde tendencies, it would help to make an understanding of probability, in its diverse authentic interpretations, part of basic general education, and certainly part of a doctor's training. For the different forms of uncertainty that enter into questions of health and sickness can easily lead to error and misjudgement.

NOTES

1 *Aphorisms from Osler's Bedside Teaching and Writings* (ed. W. B. Bean), New York: Schuman, 1950, p. 125 cited by L. B. Lusted, *Introduction to Medical Decision Making*, Springfield, Ill.: C. C. Thomas, 1968, p. 3; see also H. Hamilton, Measurement in Medicine, *New Scientist*, 1969, Vol. 44, pp. 504–5; and J. Yerushalmy *et al.*, 'An Evaluation of the Role of Serial Chest Roentgenograms in Estimating the Progress of Disease in Patients with Pulmonary Tuberculosis', *Amer. Rev. Tuber.*, 1951, Vol. 64, p. 225.

An investigation by P. J. Hoffman, P. Slovic and L. G. Rorer ('An Analysis-of-Variance Model for the Assessment of Configural Cue Utilization in Clinical Judgement', *Psychol. Bull.*, 1968, Vol. 69, pp. 338–49) reports a poor inter-judge concordance. Nine radiologists had to decide, by the presence or absence of roentological signs on the likelihood that certain ulcers were malignant. The inter-judge correlation was no more than 0·38. See also the 'Bibliography on Observer Error Studies', in L. B. Lusted, (op. cit.). Lusted attempts to adapt to the medical situation the methods developed in statistical decision and signal detection theory. I suspect, however, that he is a trifle too ready to accept the claim that it is possible, in signal detection, to obtain a measure of the observer's response which is independent of a measure of his sensitivity. Moreover, he does not really face up to the question of how decisions are actually made (by doctor or patient). Somewhat uncritically (following W. Edwards) he concentrates on how decisions should be made, and disregards the psychological complexities that inhere in attempting to 'apprehend the world by conjecture'.

The student familiar with the distinction between Type I and Type II statistical errors will readily grasp the kinds of observer error in medicine, as classified by Lusted. Type I error leads us to say that there is a difference between two classes when in fact there is not. In other words it is a wrong rejection of the null hypothesis. Type II error leads us to say that there is *no* difference when there really *is*; in this case, the null hypothesis is wrongly accepted.

These two errors correspond respectively, to the classification 'false negative' and 'false positive' in medical investigation. If a sick person is classified as healthy, this is a false negative; the null hypothesis (that all are sick) is wrongly *rejected*; If, however, a healthy person is classified as sick this is a false positive; the null hypothesis (that all are sick) is wrongly *accepted*.

Since 'positive' in medicine means disease, whereas in psychology and other spheres it may signify something useful, it would be better, in a medical context, to say 'falsely declared well' (instead of false negative), and 'falsely declared sick' (instead of false positive). 'Observer error' will be most difficult to overcome when there is an appreciable overlap, with respect to the test measurements, between the healthy (truly negative) and the sick (truly positive) populations. In such circumstances the physician's risk-taking tendencies will determine whether he wants to ensure that he identifies all the sick, even if this means also including the healthy *or* he wants to ensure that he does not make *any* 'false positives', even at the cost of making some 'false negatives'.

2   See report in *The Times*, 28 May 1968.
3   J. Hinton, 'The Special Needs of the Patient', in *People and Cancer*, London: The British Cancer Council, 1970, p. 39.
4   WHO Press Release/33, 18 December 1969,.
5   J. M. Bynner, *Medical Students' Attitudes Towards Smoking*, A report on a survey carried out for the Ministry of Health, SS382, London: H.M.S.O., 1967.
6   P. Slovic, 'Value as a Determiner of Subjective Probability', Institute of Electrical and Electronic Engineers *Transactions on Human Factors in Electronics*, 1966, Vol. HFE-7, No. 1, pp. 22–8.
7   F. P. Ramsey, 'Truth and Probability' (1926) in *The Foundations of Mathematics and Other Logical Essays* (ed. E. B. Braithwaite), New York: The Humanities Press, 1950.
8   *An Essay Concerning Human Understanding* (1690), Chap. XV.
9   Locke, op. cit. Chap. XVI.
10   C. H. Fellner and J. R. Marshall, 'Kidney Donors', in *Altruistic and Helping Behaviour*, J. Macaulay and L. Berkowitz (eds.), London: Academic Press, 1970, pp. 269–81.
11   M. Blumenthal (ed.) *The Denver Symposium on Mass Communication for Traffic Safety*, US. National Safety Council, 1964.
12   According to Dr Charles Fletcher, secretary of the committee on smoking of the Royal College of Physicians, a 35-year-old man loses about fifteen minutes of his life for every cigarette he smokes (The *Guardian*, 17 September 1970). A report *Smoking and Health Now* was published by the Royal College of Physicians in January 1971.
13   L. S. Penrose, *On the Objective Study of Crowd Behaviour*, London: H. K. Lewis, 1952.
14   J. Cohen, C. E. M. Hansel and Edith F. May, 'Natural History of Learned and Scientific Societies', *Nature*, 1954, Vol. 178, pp. 328–33.

CHAPTER 7

Uncertainty in Crime

I. *Uncertainty in the System*

The word 'crime', in strict usage, is a form of behaviour defined by legal, not by psychological or even by social criteria. A man is a criminal if a court pronounces that he is guilty of violating the criminal law. Many a man—the number is unknown—violates the law but evades detection; and a proportion of those that are charged are no doubt able, by virtue of a skilful defence, to exonerate themselves, although if the full truth were known they would be guilty. Eminent criminal lawyers readily admit that they have sometimes succeeded in getting a man acquitted on a murder charge when, in their hearts, they have believed in his guilt. It has been reliably estimated by a Deputy Commissioner of the Metropolitan Police that, in Britain, some 40 per cent of those who plead not guilty, and who resist prosecution 'by means both fair and foul', are acquitted, although most of them have, in fact, committed the offence of which they are charged.[1]

The judicial sphere offers other situations where considerable uncertainty may be present in the minds of judge and jury and yet a verdict has to be reached which is 'beyond reasonable doubt', or where there is 'a preponderance of probability'. Investigation shows that the interpretation of such legal phrases, which a judge employs in giving direction to a jury, may vary widely from one person to another. Thus, one-third of the subjects in a sample of adults studied by us regarded 'beyond reasonable doubt' as signifying a chance of seven in ten of being right, and another third believed that even a nine in ten chance allowed too much room for doubt. Clearly, therefore, there is uncertainty in the system as a whole with respect to whether an individual has committed a given crime, an uncertainty that is not dispelled by the apparent effectiveness of legal procedure. Let me first consider the offender and then pass on to the way the law deals with uncertainty.

II. *The Individual Offender*

The predicament of the offender is analogous to that of the patient. His uncertainty with respect to detection, capture, punishment and its severity is not measured by statistics based on the population of offenders, any more than a patient's uncertainty is measured by morbidity statistics. For one thing, he may not be aware of these statistics; for another, he may misinterpret them, and believe that they are not applicable to him. Nevertheless, many of those who speak for the law, including the police, are apt to believe that the statistics do represent the offender's state of mind.

By way of illustration let me quote a former Lord Chancellor, Lord Gardiner, who told a meeting of magistrates that 'if you committed robbery or assault in London today, the chances are four to one that you would not get caught'. The odds, he said, against getting caught for house-breaking were six to one; for larceny, ten to one; and for stealing from cars, thirteen to one; and 'it was the certainty of being caught, and not the severity of the punishment, that was the main deterrent to crime. If all punishment were abolished for murder, there would hardly be any increase in crime'.[2]

This statement calls for several comments.

(i) We ought to note that, in the first place, murder is in a class apart from other crimes, and while the abolition of capital punishment may not appreciably affect the homicide rate, we cannot infer from this that the abolition of punishment for other offences would likewise have little or no effect. If a man knows that he is not going to be punished, why should he care very much whether he is caught or not?

The situation is, however, not quite as simple as it may appear at first sight. Whenever public opinion runs ahead of the law and legal penalties are felt to be disproportionately severe, juries are reluctant to convict. So only a small fraction of sentences are actually implemented with full rigour, and the threat they constitute tends to lose its deterrent effect.

If, and when, penalties become more severe (as is now becoming the case, for example, for drug pushing) the potential offender is apt to harden in relation to the penalty. Terror, it has been said, has its own law of diminishing returns. When punishment is savage, people are no more put off by it than they are by a milder régime. Legal savagery begets public barbarity.

It may be true that if the punishment for an offence is suddenly made much harsher, there may be a deterrent effect for a while. But this soon wears off, and the offence rate returns gradually to its original level. I suspect that this is what is now happening with the breathalyser. If the penalty for speeding or wrong parking were to be sterilization or amputation of a limb, the number of offences might be reduced for a week or two, and then begin to mount again.

(ii) Secondly, from the context, Lord Gardiner appears to measure 'certainty' by the statistics of capture. But the offender can only be influenced by his *own* state of mind. Even if he accepted that there was a 99 per cent capture rate, he might still feel that he would be the lucky one and evade the police. Here, too, we may draw an analogy with a patient who believes that he will be the lucky '1 per cent' to survive the operation.

The belief in luck and unluck may well influence the behaviour of criminals and would be worth investigating from this point of view. There is a long tradition, still very much alive in recent centuries, to the effect that a criminal, as such, is lucky. This belief may conceivably have an ancient origin in rites at which prisoners of war and miscreants were done to death at a feast when the participants sacrificed the totem. There are reports of the ceremonial drinking of a criminal's blood. Subsequently, there are signs that the body of the criminal assumed a special significance.

We can trace, at least to Roman times, the peculiar veneration attached to the corpse of a criminal. For centuries his skin was credited with the power of assuaging the pangs of labour. It was cut into strips and converted into a 'poor sinner's ointment'.

The tremendous interest still aroused in many people by the exploits of major criminals may be a residue of the time when they were revered as heroes and almost as a species of saint. It was evidently the custom in Rome to attach the name of Hercules posthumously to a 'great' criminal, and sometimes a cult grew up about him. At all events, a widespread belief survived that everything that belongs to an executed man brings good fortune. The purse that preserves a finger or other small bone of a criminal will never be empty of coin. Vermin will be kept at a distance, and so will thieves. A household is perpetually blessed if such a bone is buried beneath its threshold; no shopkeeper could do better than preserve a thief's thumb. When the gallows at Breslau were dismantled, a lively trade was plied in the bones discovered underneath. A criminal's blood was particularly potent. It could cure various diseases and fevers, like the blood of gladiators which Roman enthusiasts imbibed against epilepsy. Gout could be kept at bay by eating bread dipped in a criminal's blood, which is more effective while still warm and fresh. The halter is also luck-bearing, and when thrice struck preserves a house from lightning. A child's scrofula could be cured by lashing the child with the hangman's rope. The criminal's fat was also sometimes in demand. At Prussian executions the crowd rushed forward with spoons and vessels to catch some of the victim's blood.[3]

In short, there was something 'divine' or rather demonic about the criminal, and by incorporating his flesh or blood one could acquire some of his power. When dead he exuded some beneficent 'substance'. According to Hartland, there was, in Sicily (home of the Mafia), a cult which worshipped the souls of dead criminals, with a church at Palermo, the *Chiesa delle Anime de' Corpi Decollati*.[4]

There is another aspect to this question of the offender's 'certainty' of capture. An eminent jurist has asserted that 'an exception merely confirms the rule'. But an offender, knowing that twenty of his fellows have been caught and that he himself has evaded capture, may regard this exception as *dis*confirming the rule, and he may be encouraged, as a result, to undertake further exploits. This illustrates, in a novel context, the phenomenon of negative recency. Evidence from our experiments suggests that two-thirds of the population may believe that an exception destroys the rule.[5]

(iii)   Thirdly, the severity of punishment, in the light of its effectiveness as a deterrent, must also be judged subjectively, that is, as it appears to the offender. For example, what is a heavy fine to one, may be negligible to another.

(iv)   Fourthly, if the psychological probability of capture and severity of punishment have an impact on the offender, it is through the interaction between them rather than through each independently of the other. We do not know what form the interaction might take in different individuals, whether, for example, it is additive or multiplicative.

Consider the following possibilities (where ψ signifies 'psychological probability of') (see Table 5).

TABLE 5   *Psychological probability of capture and degree of punishment: possible combinations*

Capture	Punishment		
$^\psi$high	$^\psi$high	severe	(1)
		mild	(2)
$^\psi$high	$^\psi$low	severe	(3)
		mild	(4)
$^\psi$low	$^\psi$high	severe	(5)
		mild	(6)
$^\psi$low	$^\psi$low	severe	(7)
		mild	(8)

A high ψ of capture plus a high ψ of a *mild* punishment may be subjectively equivalent to a low ψ of capture, with a high ψ of a *severe* punishment. Thus an individual might be indifferent to (2) and (5) in Table 5. Each of these might deter more than (3), namely, a high ψ of capture with a low ψ of a *severe* penalty.

A low ψ of capture with a low ψ of *severe* punishment, i.e. (7), might be less of a deterrent than a high ψ of capture plus a high ψ of *mild* punishment, i.e. (1).

At any given ψ of capture, a low ψ of punishment which varies in severity from case to case may be more of a deterrent than a high ψ of a *mild* penalty or a low ψ of a *severe* penalty.

In all that I have been saying so far is implied the idea that the offender is taking a gamble. He is staking his ψ of freedom of movement, and possibly his reputation, against his ψ of loot and punishment. Freedom of movement (FM) and loot (L) are positive utilities (U), while punishment (P) is a disutility $(\bar{U})$. So we may say that he is staking his $\psi(FM) \cdot U(FM)$ against his

$$\psi(L) \cdot U(L) \cdot \frac{1}{\psi(P) \cdot \bar{U}(P)}$$

This formulation assumes that the expectation of capture which enters into the offender's idea of punishment is independent of his hope that he will retain the loot. We should also allow for the possibility, however, that the essential choice confronting many an offender is not a gamble of this sort but a choice between the utility of offending and the utility of not offending.

III. *The Element of Time*

Into this situation, as in the medical, generally speaking, the more remote in time the possibility of an event, the less credibility we attach to it. Our temporal horizon seems to become less real, as judged by its impact on present decision-making, as it recedes into the subjective future. That is perhaps why many an offender against the law takes his chance; the apparent remoteness in time of a possible penalty weakens any deterrent effect it might have on him. Several factors are compounded. There is, first, the uncertainty of detection or capture. Secondly, there is the uncertainty of punishment, and of its degree of severity. We do not know how these uncertainties interact, but we may assume that even if the offender assigned a high probability to his being caught in the act, he would not necessarily hold back if the penalty, however large, seemed to him sufficiently far away in time. By contrast, a small fine for parking imposed by a traffic warden at the time of the offence might be a more potent deterrent than the possibility of an eternity in limbo, just as a transient demise for an afternoon straight after smoking a packet of cigarettes might be a stronger deterrent than horrific pictures of a distant carcinoma.

IV. *Types of Offence in Relation to Risk*

Uncertainty and risk-taking do not play a part equally in all offences. Crime cannot be treated as though it homogeneously belongs to the same psychological or social category. There are basic differences between offences. One distinction which, I suggest, might be fundamental in the present context is that between:

(i) offences against which the sanctions are external
(ii) offences against which the sanctions are internal.

For this reason, by and large—there are often complicating circumstances—questions of uncertainty and risk pertain to the first rather than to the second category. Offences in the second category, best exemplified by homicide, tend to be committed regardless of consequences or fear of identification and punishment. About 30 per cent of homicides in Britain (50 per cent, in the case of women) actually commit suicide. On the whole, only in murder linked with robbery, and in psychopathic murder, does the offender try to evade his punishment. On the other hand, in the main classes of crime against property and against the person, uncertainty and risk-taking figure prominently.

Thus the manner in which uncertainty and risk are treated, rather than respect for the law, may be crucial in distinguishing the offender from the non-offender. One could hazard the cynical hypothesis that, with respect to that class of offences for which there are external sanctions (violation of traffic laws, tax evasion, travelling on public transport without a ticket, for example), the difference between the offender and the law-abiding citizen is, in general, not that the latter is more honest, but that the former is more daring. By this I mean that, by comparison with his virtuous neighbour, he *either* attaches a lower psychological probability to the possibility of capture and punishment *or* he attaches the same probability as his neighbour does but has a different 'maximum risk-taking level'. This last expression signifies that the level of psychological probability of capture at which he is prepared to violate the law is higher than the level which his neighbour is prepared to accept. Thus, for instance, while he would be prepared to try his hand at travelling ticket-less when he thinks he has $\psi = 0{\cdot}3$ (say) of being detected, his law-abiding neighbour might require $\psi = 0{\cdot}1$.

V. *Combining Chances*

We may apply the results of experiments on 'chance' described in Chapters 2 and 3 to our present problem. For a particular feature of the manner in which uncertainty and risk may enter into crime relates to the way 'chances' are subjectively combined. In many, if not most offences, and certainly in major crimes, the illegal operation to be performed involves several distinct stages at each of which there may be a different psychological (ψ) and statistical (p) probability of capture. Two factors may distinguish the offender from the non-offender. First, he may, so to speak, process these probabilities multiplicatively rather than additively, so that the product is for that reason smaller. Secondly, he may, by comparison with others or, as judged by the statistical probability (p), underestimate the combined small probabilities at the different stages. As we have seen, for some people a single large chance is preferred to a comparatively large number of small chances, which, in combination, are mathematically preferable. For others, by contrast, two or three small chances offer a larger psychological probability than a single larger chance, although this, too, would be contrary to the mathematical expectation. The offender may belong to the former category, in that his threshold for a 'chance' is relatively high, and several small chances consequently appear to him, in the aggregate, insignificant.

However, the offender's uncertainty is not exhausted by his psychological probability of detection and punishment for which there exist (corresponding) statistical probabilities. I put 'corresponding' in parentheses because, properly speaking, the statistics of detection and punishment only 'correspond' to the offender's psychological probability in an attenuated sense. The offender may know nothing and care nothing about the statistics. In most cases he will have only the vaguest notion of what they are numerically and of what they signify. His expectation of what will happen to him may be related to knowledge of the statistics in the most tenuous fashion, and the effect of this knowledge on his behaviour may be still more tenuous.

Beyond the psychological probabilities for which we can find these so-called 'corresponding' statistics, which apply, of course, to the population of offenders, there are also psychological probabilities stemming from moral considerations. Moral aspects of crime may legitimately be considered as belonging to the domain of ethics and as being outside the scope of psychology, but, as in the case of gamblers, there might be certain moral elements in the mind of a potential offender which are an integral and perhaps a vital part of his decision-making process in relation to crime.

These elements belong to what has been known as 'moral probabilism', the idea that we should base our actions on what *we* think is probably right. In Jesuitical doctrine it is enough to be able to cite an accredited authority in support of your own views. A seventeenth-century Jesuit, Escobar, believed that a penitent had to be absolved if he believed that his action was probably right.

Havelock Ellis[6] long ago remarked—though what he says ought to be subject to further empirical test—that criminals are convinced of the criminality of the honest citizen: 'three-fourths of the social virtues are cowardly vices', said one. Another declared that 'thieving is an honourable pursuit' as compared, for example, with patriotism —'the idolatory of an idea, in the stupid worship of which the peace of the world, and the well-being of its inhabitants, were sacrificed by the law-makers and others who profit thereby'.

VI. *Further Research*

I make no claim to have attempted a comprehensive treatment of the problems raised by uncertainty in the administration of the law, civil or criminal. Such a task would be beyond the scope of this book. Many challenging questions face the future investigator. In this connection the study of testimony,[7] which has a long tradition, to which mathematicians, lawyers and psychologists have contributed, is of particular interest. Two topics seem to me specially worthy of attention. One is the study of methods of interrogation of suspects and witnesses, which could be given a 'new look' if treated as a search task. Official guidance given in Britain in the Judges' Rules (*Judges' Rules and Administrative Directions to the Police*, London, HMSO) is only of the vaguest kind, and provides no assistance whatever for the actual procedure of questioning. My own tentative enquiries suggest that the police do not use anything like a binary strategy of interrogation in which half of the possible 'items' are eliminated by each Yes-No question. Such a procedure might not be generally appropriate. The method police do seem to favour is what might be called a 'pyramidal strategy' of interrogation. This means that the first approach is made on the broadest possible front, and the range of questions progressively narrowed until the decisive question is reached. The reverse procedure, which would rely on luck in hitting on the crucial question, is considered 'stupid' by some Chief Constables, as is also an impatient 'jumping' over several interrogatory stages in order to arrive at the target question quickly. What we need to determine is the range of actual interrogatory strategies, and the optimal strategy in different circumstances.

A second topic worth pursuing is that of 'risk'. Many methods have been suggested for measuring risk but few have been shown to have any validity. So-called 'tests' of risk-taking are very dubious since there is no evidence that the tests have any application beyond the highly specific situation to which they refer. Nothing is easier than to asesmble a set of questions and call it a 'test' of this, that or the other. This procedure begs the essential question. I have elsewhere[8] discussed risk-taking in a variety of situations, so I shall limit myself here to what appear to be the measures that might profitably be used in the study of risk.

(i) The simplest measure may be obtained by asking the subject how many times he thinks he will succeed in n attempts at a given task. The task may be presented at varying levels of difficulty. The subject's estimate, which may be regarded as his assessment of the hazard (i.e. event probability), may be expressed on a scale ranging from 0 to 1·0. Call this R.

(ii) The maximum risk-taking level ($MRTL$) is the estimate of success at a task at the most difficult level which the subject is prepared to undertake. $MRTL$ varies with the utility of the outcome, and may be a function of the incentive.

(iii) The risk preferred (RP) is that level of uncertainty of success which is normally preferred. The question remains open whether this is a general, a group, or a specific factor.

(iv) A 'coefficient of safety' for each subject may be obtained by taking the difference between a measure of the most difficult level of the task he will undertake and a measure of the most difficult level at which he believes he will always be successful.

(v) A 'coefficient of hazard' may be obtained by taking the difference between the most difficult level of the task which the subject will attempt and the most difficult level at which he always succeeds.

(vi) A 'coefficient of confidence' may be obtained by taking the difference between the most difficult level at which the subject believes he will always succeed and the most difficult at which he does, in fact, always succeed.[9]

In view of the fact that traffic offences in which alcohol is involved constitute such a considerable social and legal problem, I would add a brief word on what seems to be the effect of alcohol on driving behaviour. On the basis of the measures indicated above, alcohol, within the limits studied (up to six whiskies,) appears to have little effect on risk as such. That is to say, the effect of alcohol is not to induce the driver to drive his vehicle when his estimate of success is less than what it is when he is sober. Its effect is to make him attach this estimate of success to a more difficult task, for example, to drive through a narrower gap. In other words his psychological probability of success is unchanged but it becomes associated with a greater hazard. When the intake of alcohol exceeds six whiskies, the effect might be different.

VII. *Concluding Reflections*

I end this short chapter on a historical note suggested by Huizinga.[10] He observes that doubts about a man's responsibility for his crime were unknown in the Middle Ages. They were unknown because the Middle Ages lacked our contemporary conviction that, in permitting the conditions under which crime thrives, society is itself the accomplice of the criminal. In the same way, the Middle Ages knew nothing of our wish to reclaim and rehabilitate rather than inflict a penalty or exact retribution. Yet the sentiment which inspires our relative leniency to the criminal was not wholly absent from medieval society. It was manifested in another manner. In place of mild punishment which we hesitantly impose, the Middle Ages either demanded the extreme penalty allowed by the law or was stirred by pity for the condemned. But medieval compassion has little in common with our acknowledgement of diminished responsibility or with our recognition of extenuating circumstances. No one is *entitled* to mercy, which is gratuitous, 'like the gentle rain from heaven'. There is nothing gracious in our gnawing doubt as to the criminals' culpability or as to the penalty he should suffer. Our uncertainties grow from our more lucid conception of a justice which can only be understood in the light of man's nature. Medieval mercy was religious, our doubts are scientific. In so far as the application of science is less inconstant than the fickle practice of a creed, the criminal has everything to gain from a change to law tempered by scientific understanding.

NOTES

1 R. Mark, 'A Police Point of View', *Medico-Legal Journal*, 1970, Vol. 38, pp. 4–14.
2 The *Guardian*, 22 April 1968.
3 H. Ellis, *The Criminal*, London: Walter Scott, 1890, pp. 283–5.
4 E. S. Hartland, 'The Cult of Executed Criminals at Palermo', *J. Amer. Folk-Lore*, 1910, Vol. 21, pp. 168–79.
5 J. Cohen, P. Cooper and P. Thorne, Les degrés d'évidence, *J. de Psychologie*, July-September 1962, pp. 225–8.
6 Ellis, op. cit.
7 See, for example, *J. Soc. Iss.*, 1957, Vol. 13, which is devoted to papers on 'Witnesses and Testimony at Trials and Hearings'.
8 See, for example, the chapter entitled 'Hazard and Risk on the Road' in J. Cohen and B. Preston, *Causes and Prevention of Road Accidents*, London: Faber & Faber, 1968; and the chapter on 'Risk-taking' in J. Cohen and I. Christensen, *Information and Choice*, Edinburgh: Oliver and Boyd, 1970. On the question of risk-taking in sport, see also M. Bouet, 'L'Attrait du risque chez les sportifs', *Psychol. Francaise*, 1969, Vol. 14 (2), pp. 127–34.
9 For the form the three coefficients take in the study of driving behaviour see J. Cohen, C. E. M. Hansel and E. J. Dearnaley, 'The Risk taken in Driving under the influence of Alcohol', *Brit. Med. J.*, 1958, (i) pp. 1438–42.
10 J. Huizinga, *The Waning of the Middle Ages*, London: Arnold, 1937, p. 16.

CHAPTER 8

Chance and Doubt in Art and Love

I. *Preamble*

A museum is a treasure house of a past long lost. We enter and gaze in awe at the venerable legacy of exhibits: skulls, mummies, flints, weapons, implements and ornaments hundreds, thousands, perhaps tens of thousands of years old. But we do not need to visit a museum to catch a glimpse of our past. We carry the past with us in our heads. I do not mean that we have a store of innate ideas or immutable traits which we have inherited from our remote ancestors, but that from infancy onwards, we look at the world around us, and interpret what we see, partly in the same way as they did. Otherwise primordial beliefs, in the supernatural for example, would not survive with so much force today, even in countries where the culture is largely based on science and technology. Of course, it goes without saying that cultural influences, within the home, at school and elsewhere, permeate this way of looking at things to such an extent, and to such a depth, that it is almost impossible to disentangle the influences from the different sources or to extract any feature which is totally 'culture-free'. Nevertheless, there is at least one fundamental and universal mode of interaction with the external world which overrides class or cultural differences. I have in mind the 'intuitive' infra-structure of the ideas of possibility, chance and probability. As we have seen, this infra-structure may have a biological counterpart in the 'statistical causality' which characterizes animal behaviour. Fraught with uncertainty as the human situation invariably is, some expression of the reaction to, and interpretation of, this uncertainty must, I suggest, be encountered at all times and everywhere. Indeed the ubiquitous practice of divination in archaic and ancient society, which is essentially a device for coping with uncertainty, attests to this, as do our modern divinatory techniques of statistical prediction and 'futurology'.

II. *Explanatory Use of the Idea of Chance*

So deeply ingrained is our uncertainty with respect to the things we wish to understand, that we are apt, evidently, to project it and endow it with an independent existence of its own, which we designate 'chance'. Hence ethnologists have persuaded themselves that they see traces of the magic hand of chance in the history of culture, while historians of science have convinced themselves that the same influence is at work in scientific and medical discovery and invention. How did our primeval ancestors hit upon the all-important discovery of fire? The stock answer is that one of them, by sheer good luck, happened to lick his fingers after rescuing a roast pig from a bushfire. Thenceforward deliberate conflagrations were made but on a more modest scale. Much the same line of reasoning seems to be followed in accounting for the origin of the wheel, pottery-making and other features of early civilization.

In arguing against this conception of the origin of culture, Lévi-Strauss[1] merely replaces simple chance by compound chance. Far too many independent elements were involved, he maintains, in pottery-making (for example), for them to be explained by simple chance. He therefore takes the view that the invention of pottery, like the neolithic revolution ten thousand years ago and the industrial revolution two hundred years ago, was the result of a relatively improbable sequence or combination of events. An advance in civilization is analogous, he supposes, to guessing a long series of numbers at roulette. It is a question of compound probability. He hastens to add, properly if I may say so, that the complexity of human history is such that there may be many quite different special sequences of events, each valued by a particular society. And so what the West regards as scientific progress was preordained by the cultural mood of the peoples of the West, shaped as it was by manifold influences during the Roman occupation, and over the Dark and Middle Ages.

We meet a similar situation in the history of science. Taton,[2] for instance, has shown how, again and again, an utterly unexpected and fortuitous event has proved decisive in the course of scientific discovery, but only when the discoverer was ready for it. Pasteur's oft quoted remark 'Chance favours the prepared mind' is the key to this phenomenon. Countless apples have fallen on countless heads, but it needed the head of a Newton, who had long and deeply pondered on the subject, to see in the fall of the legendary apple a principle of epoch-making significance. In discussing the role played by chance in discovery, Taton rightly distinguishes (p. 79) between 'psychological chance' and 'external chance', though his conception of 'psychological chance' as consisting of 'intuition' coupled with 'aesthetic sense', is somewhat vague.[3]

III.   *Doubt in Drama and Art*

I have been speaking so far of the role we attribute to chance when our knowledge of a set of circumstances falls short of what we should dearly like to know. Such attribution occurs typically when we are in doubt. Let us look a little more closely at this state of mind.

A man in doubt hesitates, and consequently delays reaching a decision or committing himself to action, while the degree of his doubt may affect the nature of his decision or action, making it half-hearted or whole-hearted, as the case may be. It may also reflect the emotional basis, if any, of his convictions. There may be, I suggest, an inverse relation between the emotional intensity with which a belief is held and the degree of doubt which is associated with it. When doubt enters, emotion departs, and vice versa. A man, moreover, may be ambivalent in relation to his own doubt. *Should* he be in doubt? he asks himself. And while, perhaps, at one moment he is at his wits end to exorcise it, at the next he does all he can to preserve it. Indecisiveness as such, *la folie de doute*, and obsessively deferred decision-making, belong to psychopathology.

Nearly everyone must doubt something, and concede, if only reluctantly and grudgingly, that he cannot always and everywhere make categorical assertions backed by a feeling of absolute certainty. Some speak buoyantly and with confident assurance, on matters political; others with equal certainty, about God, sport, morality, the economy of the country or the weather. Whether the tendency to doubt is a general characteristic of an individual, entering into all he thinks and making him 'a doubting Thomas', or whether it makes its appearance only with respect to some particular situation of groups of situations, is itself open to doubt and the problem may be related to the question whether risk-taking is a general, group or specific factor (see p. 118).

In the realm of theology we might do worse than contemplate the design of a Theological Barometer, as advocated by Gibbon, who suggested that a Cardinal Baronius and a Dr Middleton 'should constitute the opposite and remote extremities, as the former sunk to the lowest degree of credulity, which was compatible with learning, and the latter rose to the highest pitch of scepticism, in any wise consistent with Religion'.[4]

A function of many religious cults is to protect a man from particular forms of doubt. On this assurance of the absence of doubt rests the security and authority of the priesthood. Never must the worm of scepticism be allowed to crawl in. Ahriman, Principle of Darkness, in the Persian myth, springs from a doubt in the mind of Ormuzd, Principle of Light. Job's tribulations are the consequence of doubt which Satan insidiously plants in his mind. A ninth-century Zen Buddhist writes: 'He (the Master) . . . exploded my lump of doubt, completely to pieces.'

There are creeds which codify every imaginable human contingency, so that no one need ever hesitate, vacillate or waver in doubt throughout his waking hours. The order in which the shoes must be put on and the order in which the nails of the fingers must be trimmed, all this is laid down, there being one order for the right hand and another order for the left. Every trifling act or incident has becomes fraught with tremendous significance, because of the total submission on which the gods of the superstitious man always insist. Any event which is exceptional or seemingly violates the 'laws of nature' carries foreboding. Where this protective function usurps its other functions, the inevitable result is religious bigotry and fanaticism.

It is one thing, however, to establish the categories or qualities of doubt, to trace its multifarious sources, or to attempt to measure its infinite grades and shades of intensity, and it is another thing to determine its effect in drama, art, religion or love. I do not think tension, as induced by a Hitchcock film, is quite the same as true drama. In the former, as in detective tales, once you know whether the intending assassin is to succeed in luring his unsuspecting victim to his death, you are apt to lose interest. In drama, the intrinsic uncertainty has a curious way of surviving our knowledge of the way the plot unfolds. It is true, as Dürenmatt remarks, that if there may be a touch of arsenic in a cup of coffee which a character is about to sip, the situation will bear an element of drama for the viewer. But the viewer will lose interest when he knows whether the cup has or has not been drained. The dramatic character of *Macbeth* rests on more robust foundations.

This poses the wider question of the extent to which our appreciation of art, music as well as of drama, depends upon the unexpected or improbable. Excessive familiarity, it is true, even with the greatest works of literature and music, can bring satiety; contemporary experiments with electronic and other novel forms of musical composition and execution might, as Georges Friedmann has said, be the consequence of satiation with classical works, the result of several decades of music ceaselessly transmitted by radio. Yet there is no intrinsic incompatibility between the predictable and the aesthetic. We can listen attentively to a Beethoven sonata, or re-read *King Lear*, without feeling bored, even though we know precisely which note or line is coming next. The very familiarity may *add* to our enjoyment; while effects of fluctuation in the listener's mood may be a more potent factor than familiarity as such.

In contemporary experiments in drama, audience participation, 'happenings' and improvization, chance looms large. There was a time, however, when acting meant an acrobatic performance according to prescribed rules. The actor of today now entrusts himself to a director whose task it is to select from all the vast number of possible permutations of movement, gesture, voice or sound one which is '*brought together by chance*', and, in so doing, he succeeds in offering the most felicitous, if haphazard, juxtaposition of aesthetic properties. That is why the director has been called by Urbani[5] 'the great demiurge of chance', in cinema and theatre alike. In the ordered theatre of bygone days, the director had no place; now he seems to count more than the actor or author, even if the author is Shakespeare himself. A director is 'A photographer without a camera . . . (who) shakes things out of the lethargy of their own objectivity'.

Much the same may be said about certain trends in pictorial art. Urbani sees the origin of the abstract movement in Marcel Duchamp's 'ready mades' and in the *papiers dechirés* of Jean Arp, one of whose works is entitled 'Rectangles arranged according to the Laws of Chance' (1916). In such experiments, the subject-matter is presented as if it lacked a context of causality and as if it were torn out of the objective order of things.

A similar ordered disorder is the hallmark of the furniture that invades the homes of the affluent middle classes. Time and space are homogenized in the magpie collection from this period and that, from this country and that. Pseudo-Georgian pieces reside uneasily with Edwardian and Victorian relics, enlivened by a Danish coffee-table made from teak imported from Indo-China. All is assembled under the benign rule of the 'law of chance'.

IV. *Uncertainty in Love*

Coquetry, the flight from the male and the return, the running away in circles, the 'game of yes and no', as Remy de Gourmont calls it, at once so cruel and so amorous, all this is not peculiar to the human female. For sound biological reasons it appears in many species of animals. Doubt, rather than music, is the food of love. Hence the antithesis often drawn between the poetry of romance and the prose of marriage; the former must wane and die for the latter to prosper. They cannot coexist simultaneously, for romance is nourished by uncertainty, whereas marriage rests on repetitive achievement. What counts in romantic love, is the chase and the hunt, not capture and possession. Perhaps we have an analogue here with the 'change of sign' in the gambler's relation to his prize (see p. 70). It is unthinkable that Isolde should ever really become the wife of Tristan, Juliet the wife of Romeo, or Cleopatra the wife of Anthony. Unattainability enhances desirability. Remove the barrier and the objective loses its appeal. 'Now', says Henri de Marsay (in Balzac's *The Girl with the Golden Eyes*) 'that I know this beautiful girl (Paquita), this masterpiece of nature, is mine, the adventure has lost its charm'.

In the Age of Chivalry, romance yearns for that which is out of reach; the lady-love of the gallant knight must always be the wedded wife of another.[6] Love and marriage are antipodes. So much so that as late as the sixteenth century Montaigne dares to say that 'it is a kind of incest to employ, in this venerable and sacred parentage (i.e. marriage) the efforts and extravagances of amorous licence'.[7]

The essential antithesis between medieval romance and marriage is caught in a question brought before a Court of Love, in 1176, by a baron and lady of Champagne. Is love compatible with marriage? 'No', says the baron, 'I admire and respect the sweet intimacy of married couples, but I cannot call it love. Love desires obstacles, mystery, stolen favours. Now husbands and wives boldly avow their relationship; they possess each other without contradiction and without reserve. It cannot then be love that they experience.' After due deliberation the ladies of the Court accepted the baron's verdict.[8]

The agony of uncertainty in love is nowhere more poignantly depicted than in the immortal tale of Tristan and Isolde. There is an episode in which Tristan, by force of remarkable circumstances, is compelled to abandon his mistress, Queen Isolde, the wife of King Mark, and become the husband of another Isolde, (or Ysolt) of the White Hands. The moment of truth arrives when he is called upon to perform his husbandly duties whereupon he finds himself landed in a classical 'approach-avoidance' situation.

'How can I do it?' he says to himself. 'This deed is repugnant to me. Nevertheless I must lie down as with my lawful wife. I am bound to lie with her, for I am unable to desert her . . . how this grieves me! I have married her lawfully at the church door in the sight of the people. I can by no means repulse her, but must now commit an act of folly. I cannot hold aloof from this girl without great sin and misdemeanour. Nor can I unite with her, unless I mean to perjure myself for I am so committed to the other Isolde that it would be wrong for this Ysolt to have me. I owe so much to this Ysolt that I cannot keep faith with another and I must not break faith again, nor may I abandon this one! If I ever have my pleasure with any other, I shall be breaking my faith with Isolde my beloved, and if I depart from this Ysolt, then I shall commit a sin, and evil and wrong. For I may neither leave her nor take my pleasure of her by lying with her in her bed for my profit and delight. Indeed, I am so committed to the Queen that I must not lie with this girl, and am so committed to this girl that I cannot possibly retreat. I must neither betray Isolde nor yet abandon my wife, I may neither separate from her nor may I lie with her. If I keep my promise to this girl, I shall break my vow to Isolde; and if I keep faith with Isolde, I shall break faith with my wife. But I must not break faith with her nor will I act against Ysolt. I do not know to which I should be false, since I must trick, betray, and deceive one, or, so it seems, play false to both together! For this girl has come so close to me that Isolde is already betrayed. I have loved the Queen so much that the girl is betrayed, and I, too, am greatly betrayed. Unlucky was I to know either! Each suffers because of me, and I suffer for two Ysolts at once . . . I have broken faith with the Queen and cannot keep it with this girl for whom I had to break it. Now, I can keep it towards one of them, and since I have already broken faith with the Queen, I must keep faith with the girl, for I cannot leave her. Nor must I betray Isolde'.[9]

Tristan's distress is not due to uncertainty about the Queen's love for him, and he is sure, as well, of the love of the other Ysolt. His doubt springs from this dilemma: given that he is loved by both, and can yield to one of them only by sacrificing the other, which he cannot contemplate, what can he do? This predicament dramatizes a situation which is not uncommon. But in our humdrum world, uncertainty in love more usually assumes the kind of form described, two thousand years ago, by Lucretius: 'All (effort) is in vain, since out of the very well-spring of delights rises up something bitter . . . because she has launched forth some word and left its meaning *in doubt*'[10] (my italics).

Proust hits the same nail on the head. The lover, he observes, is less often moved to passion by charm than by some such remark as—'I'm afraid I'm not free this evening'. Doubt, he goes on, endows those we love with 'a quality which surpasses even beauty; which is one of the reasons why we see men who are indifferent to the most beautiful women fall passionately in love with others who appear to us ugly'.[11] Thus we have the basis of what Maurois calls the 'Proustian law': Love can survive possession, can even grow, so long as it still carries an element of doubt.

Fable has something to contribute to our topic. The darts of Cupid fly at random, which may represent a belief that chance decides who is to couple with whom. A redundancy is built into this fable, for Cupid is blind. This makes it doubly sure that the arrows wantonly find their targets. With the same thought in mind, we say that marriage is a lottery, which is possibly the symbolic meaning of a love potion. Tristan—and is there not a little Tristan in every man?— might just as well have become enamoured of any other woman, and Isolde for any other man. As Auden once said, they are not in the slightest degree interested in each other as individuals. They are attracted as by a magnet, and might just as well have drawn each other's names out of a hat. Chance which binds, if not blinds, a man to a particular woman for life, might equally well have harnessed him to any one of a hundred thousand others. The collision of lovers, in short, is sheer contingency.

The apparently capricious and fortuitous character of 'falling in love' is associated with another feature—its suddenness. The arrows of Cupid come like 'a bolt from the blue'. Sometimes, these arrows, so the Greeks believed, are poisoned, a belief which conveys the notion that love can be a mysterious affliction and, like all diseases, a penalty imposed by the retributive gods.

NOTES

1 Claude Levi-Strauss, *Race and History*, UNESCO, pp. 31–8.
2 R. Taton, *Reason and Chance in Scientific Discovery*, London: Hutchinson, 1957.
3 See the discussion of chance in 'creativity' in my *Homo Psychologicus*, London: Allen & Unwin, 1971.
4 Keynes, op. cit. p. 21.
5 G. Urbani, 'The Role of Chance in Today's Art, *Diogenes*, 1962, pp. 112–30.
6 Denis de Rougemont, *Passion and Society*, London: Faber & Faber, 1956.
7 *Essays*, Book i, 29; Book iii, 5.
8 E. de la Bedollière, *Histoire des moeurs des Francais*, Vol. iii, p. 334 (quoted by H. Ellis, VI, pp. 516–17.
9 *Tristran* of Thomas of Britain (*c.* 1165), Harmondsworth: Penguin Books, 1960, pp. 307–8.
10 *De Natura Rerum*, Book IV.
11 A. Maurois, *The Quest for Proust*, (trans. G. Hopkins), London: Cape, 1950, p. 217.

An Etymological Note on 'Chance'

Chambers' *Etymological Dictionary*[1] defines 'chance' (Lat. *cadere*, to fall) as 'that which falls out or happens without assignable cause: an unexpected event: risk: opportunity: possibility: probability. From the same Latin root comes 'casual', in the sense of accidental or unforseen, and 'case' in the sense of that which falls or happens.

According to Partridge[2] the Latin *cadere* is akin to the Sanskrit root *cad* = to fall, and to the *kad* of Greek *kekadonto*, they have yielded.

On the other hand, Urbani suggests that the Greeks employed *automaton* to denote 'the true meaning of chance' as a response on the part of *x* to something totally extraneous to the system of which *x* is a part. *Automaton* consists of two words: *auto* = self, and *maton*, from *maomai* = to wish, to seek. The root of *maomai* may be *men*, which is cognate with the English *man*, and with the German *Mann*, through a common derivation from Sanskrit *matah* = thought. Compare Latin *mens*, mind, and *memini*, I remember: Gk. *mimnesko*.

Maomai signifies a seeking for something which is, in a sense, remembered. At the same time it conveys the precariousness of this search which is motivated possibly even more by the desire to remember than by the remembrance itself. Thus *automaton* is that which seeks itself. We may accordingly say that to ascribe something to 'chance' is to say that it struggles not to return to that from which it has fallen.

NOTES

1 Chambers' *Etymological Dictionary*, Edinburgh: Chambers, 1959.
2 E. Partridge, *Origins*, London: Routledge & Kegan Paul, 1958.

Epilogue

In bringing this introduction to 'perceptive probability' to a close, let us try and see it in perspective, in relation to certain historical issues raised at the Niels Bohr Institute's Symposium on Statistical Causality.

One may venture the suggestion that the self-same experiences which give rise to intuitions of chance and probability inspired the pre-Socratic philosophers, of the sixth century BC, to speculate on the nature of the universe. For lack of physics and any empirical psychology, these ancient thinkers were metaphysicians. They sought to establish the laws which govern natural phenomena, and were not concerned with the mental processes of the individual. The issues were polarized: being *v.* becoming; determinism *v.* contingency; timelessness *v.* change.

We owe to Parmenides the most daring expression of the philosophy of 'being', while Heraclitus represents the philosophy of 'becoming'.

A fragment attributed to Parmenides of Elea gives the gist of his conception of a universe which is timeless, and hence without contingency, chance, or change: 'what is uncreated and indestructible; for it is complete, immovable, and without end. Nor was it ever, nor will it be; for now it is, all at once a continuous one. . . . Thus is becoming extinguished and passing away not to be heard of. Nor is it divisible, since it is all alike. . . .'[1]

This is the earliest statement of *static monism*. If there is an infinite chain of cause and effect, time and succession are an illusion. Past, present and future are no more than aspects of an omnipresent which, to our limited consciousness, seem a sequence of states. On this view, the universe is a vast, petrified museum in which there can be neither change nor succession nor contingency.

Metaphysicians, ancient and modern, attempt to construct a rational scheme of things. The study of perceptive probability has the more modest aim of describing how men in general use the categories of determinism and contingency in their interpretation of themselves, their own conduct, the thoughts and actions of others, and the phenomena of inanimate nature.

The relevant questions are clustered in such a way that to unravel one is not necessarily to find a clue to others. We are capable of 'holding' views which seem, even to ourselves, logically incompatible. For instance, I may believe that I am 'free' in the choices I make, and yet I may at the same time be convinced that all my choices are determined. For I find it almost impossible to understand how any thought or action of mine can be undetermined. Thus I hold simultaneously two beliefs which nevertheless appear to me to be mutually contradictory. The flaws in this train of thought, from the point of view of logic, do not prevent people from thinking in this way. The existence of logic is no guarantee that its rules will not be ignored or flouted, any more than the existence of medical science ensures that people will never fall ill.

The ancient enigma—if all is determined how is true change possible?—puzzled the scholastics too, and they resolved it by taking refuge in the invocation of time. 'The Schoolmen', wrote Hobbes,[2] 'taught that "the Future is the cause of all things". That is, they gave a name to their ignorance of causes.' The Eleatics would say that to treat chance as cause is simply substituting another name for ignorance of causes.

It is of some interest to note that many of our adolescents today are Schoolmen at heart, for they too identify contingency with future time. If we ask them to distinguish between past and future, this is what they typically say: 'The future is uncertain and difficult to predict, whereas the past is certain'; 'The future, unlike the past, is new, novelty occurs in the future'; 'Mistakes can be made in the future but we cannot make mistakes in the past'; 'The past is concrete and real, but the future is abstract and unreal'; 'The past is stationary but we are always moving into the future'; 'The future exerts more influence on the present than the past does.'

Perhaps we should recognize two modes of explanation, one assigning an event to a rational context; the other allowing fortuitous events which belong to no context. The former is causal, the latter casual. Something *caused*, whether by strict determinism or statistically, is, in principle, predictable, inevitable and expected; something *casual* is unpredictable, capricious and unexpected. A bridge between the two modes may be formed by introducing an element of contingency into cause, in other words, by statistical causality, which permits chance to attenuate a rigid determinism. Something *might* happen; on the other hand, it might not. There is only a probability that the event in question will occur. If the probability is unspecified, we call it a 'possibility'. The situation is at once causal and casual.

In the last resort, a justification for the study of perceptive probability may be found in the fact man engages, doubtfully, in many activities, and these are not well understood. Man supposes, guesses, and reasons; he makes estimates and inferences. He extrapolates and interpolates. He tends to generalize and make deductions. He takes risks and arrives at decisions in the light of partial information. He has dispositions and preferences. He has to deal with unique, non-repeatable as well as with repeatable situations. He has to argue from evidence to conclusion; he has to test his private hypotheses. And he has to act. This spectrum of human conjecture provides a rationale for the further study of psychological probability.

NOTES

1 J. Burnet, *Early Greek Philosophy*, London: A. & C. Black, 1930, fourth edition, pp. 174–5 (first published 1892).
2 *The Leviathan* (1651), London: Dent, Everyman edition, p. 371.

Index